Hands off - it's my go!
IT in the languages classroom

Terry Atkinson

With contributions by

Christine Quantrell, *Planning for IT*

Michèle Deane, *Databases and concept keyboards*

Published jointly by

First published 1992
Copyright © 1992 Centre for Information on Language Teaching and Research
ISBN 1 874016 15 1

Cover by Logos Design & Advertising
Printed in Great Britain by Multiplex Medway Ltd

Published jointly by Centre for Information on Language Teaching and Research,
Regent's College, Inner Circle, Regent's Park, London NW1 4NS and National Council
for Educational Technology, Sir William Lyons Road, Science Park, Coventry CV4 7EZ.

Contents

Foreword

The National Curriculum for Modern Foreign Languages provides a challenge for pupils and teachers alike. The emphasis on skills and processes in Part 1 of the Programmes of Study forces us to look not just at how we teach but at how pupils learn. The entitlement of all pupils to a rich and stimulating experience using a variety of approaches and activities was pivotal to the philosophy of the Modern Foreign Languages Working Group. So, too, was the provision of opportunities for learners to use and respond to language through their own interests. The Levels and Statements of Attainment oblige us to address questions of progression and differentiation across all four skills. Consequently, teachers must re-evaluate their classroom practice in order to provide a wide range of appropriately targeted experiences for pupils.

This book explores how Information Technology will support both teachers and pupils in responding to that challenge. It meets the needs of the novice as well as of the experienced IT user. It gives a wealth of examples of IT in the classroom and also tackles the question of planning and integration into the scheme of work and into the whole school IT policy.

Terry Atkinson and his team of contributors have their feet firmly planted on the ground. All examples and suggestions are based on current experience, practice and research. The day to day realities of access to IT are also addressed. Whilst reassuring the timid IT user, the book will also provide inspiration for the confident practitioner as well as persuasive arguments for the sceptic. 'Hands off - it's my go!' may then indeed become the classroom quote of the nineties - in the target language, of course!

Mary Ryan
Adviser for Modern Languages, County of Avon
Member of the Modern Foreign Languages National Curriculum Working Group

April 1992

Preface

Today, developments in Information Technology (IT) proceed relentlessly.

- A single CD (compact disc) holds the equivalent text and graphics of books occupying five metres of shelving, and costs as little as £1.00 to produce; it can also store video and sound.
- 'Max', a computerised database about the European Community, can understand your spoken enquiry in French, German and English and speak the answer (telephone 'Max' on 0800 299 635).
- Palmtop computers - such is miniaturisation! - contain the same computing power as a machine which occupied a whole room 20 years ago, yet cost 1% of their price.

Developments like these (which within two years will be as routinely accepted and used as calculators), together with concepts such as virtual reality, a digital world and telecommuting prove that there is no shortage of new terms or of disquieting facts to shake our notions about learning, working, text, information and communication.

Having, over the past decade, slowly come to grips with more conventional computer-assisted language learning (CALL) applications in the form of vocabulary acquisition, text-handling and other dedicated software programs, modern language teachers still feel left behind by this pace of change. It is hardly surprising then that a 1991 DES survey revealed that 65% of modern languages teachers said they felt they lacked confidence in using IT.

By contrast, the IT skills casually and routinely demonstrated by youngsters (often the very pupils who find learning a language so difficult) add to the disorientation of teachers. On television recently, an eighteen-month-old child used a computer-input device, known as a mouse, to draw pictures, while ten-year-olds in primary school are at ease with the integrated software handled by their parents at work (who are presumably not teachers!).

In school today, in many countries, efforts are being made to update the curriculum to include IT skills, both to prepare young people for the technologically based environment they are likely to work in, and to enable the benefits of technology to be applied to the learning process. However, it is only the National Curriculum of England and Wales that expects all teachers to be, in effect, teachers of IT, since legislation requires that Technology Attainment Target 5 (Information Technology) be taught and assessed within other subjects.

Furthermore, the National Curriculum Order for Modern Foreign Languages includes the statutory entitlement that in schools *'all pupils should have regular opportunities to use computers'*. As one teacher has said: *'Am I a good teacher if I don't use IT?'* The answer has to be: *'Of course you are!'*, but many other teachers and pupils have found that IT, appropriately used, can have profound benefits in learning a language.

For modern language teachers, one issue that arises from IT in the National Curriculum is this. Whereas emphasis is placed on open-ended IT tools like word processors and spreadsheets across all phases and all subjects, those applications are played down for which dedicated CALL programs like *Granville* and *Fun with Texts* were specifically developed. As these have often been language teachers' first contact with IT and what they have exploited most successfully, it is surprising that the National Curriculum does not appear to endorse their use.

In fact, the Order and the Non-Statutory Guidance for Modern Foreign Languages do not exclude them. The basic position in the Programmes of Study is that pupils should be helped by all appropriate means to achieve linguistic competence and that *'pupils should have regular opportunities to use computers'* as one way of achieving that aim. However, packages designed for a specific purpose are usually self-explanatory and are becoming ever more user-friendly, whereas more exemplification and guidance is needed in the effective use of open-ended software. This reflects the typical development in use of IT by teachers as they begin with 'dedicated' software, go on to explore applications which offer more scope for authoring and learner-autonomy, and eventually produce their own resources to suit their way of teaching and their students' needs. In the process, they become aware of more open-ended IT tools and duly integrate them into their learning programmes.

This book refers to 'IT in language learning' rather than 'computer-assisted language learning' in order to reflect the thinking behind the National Curriculum. However, the difference is mainly of terminology rather than of practice. IT should only be used in language learning when it assists, therefore all appropriate uses of IT in language learning can be termed CALL.

The ideas contained in the following pages will help to show the wealth of language learning activities that can be devised using only one or two pieces of open-ended software. At the same time, they will enable pupils to broaden their IT experience and link language lessons with what is going on in other curriculum areas. Inevitably, the actual software and machines used will change in time, but the principles will hold good.

The National Council for Educational Technology commissioned Terry Atkinson of Bristol University to write a book that would help modern linguists feel more at ease using IT in language lessons. He has based it on his experience working with students and teachers in the south-west (and consequently the machines and software used by them). He also included contributions from a number of leading practitioners involved in NCET curriculum development projects; these are intended to provide support to those seeking to take the first steps in using IT and to those wishing to extend their use of IT in appropriate ways. One or two of the case studies have appeared in other publications, but it was felt right to reproduce them in collected form in this joint CILT/ NCET publication. Unlike previous NCET and CILT publications, the pages of this book, text and graphics, were desktop published by Terry himself using *PageMaker*, thus practically demonstrating the enabling power of the present generation of IT tools at our disposal.

In Chapter 2, Christine Quantrell comments that *'the best uses of IT in language learning will be conceived by the best teachers of languages'*. This serves to remind us that we should not be overawed by technological developments or enticed into buying overhyped products of dubious quality simply because they are on CD-ROM and are computer- rather than paper-based. Without doubt, they can offer genuine advances in learning. Nevertheless, we should appropriate and tailor them for our own purposes and not be afraid of rejecting those which we instinctively feel do not support good practices in language learning.

From our discussions with language teachers, it is clear that two factors are crucial in moving forward with IT: gaining confidence in using the equipment and seeing how colleagues use IT. This book, in conjunction with other materials available from CILT, NCET and others, is designed to help on both counts. It may be read from cover to cover by newcomers to IT to raise their awareness and learn how to plan for IT; it may also serve as a resource and source of reference and ideas to be consulted at leisure by those who are already familiar with IT and who seek to widen their experience.

If, after reading the book, the reader asks *'Why should I **not** use IT?'* then we shall have achieved our aim.

Roger Blamire, NCET
Eric Brown, CILT
March 1992

Notes on contributors

Mary Ryan is Adviser for Modern Languages for the County of Avon and was a member of the modern foreign languages working group which prepared the initial advice and the final report on the National Curriculum.

Roger Blamire is a Curriculum Officer for the National Council for Educational Technology with special responsibility for modern languages.

Eric Brown is now in his second spell at CILT and has been another very influential figure in the world of IT in modern languages through his writing and thinking on the subject and through the annual CILT conferences in Lancaster.

Michèle Deane is a Lecturer in Education and Modern Languages at the University of Bath School of Education.

Christine Quantrell is a Lecturer in Education and Modern Languages at Portsmouth Polytechnic School of Education and an Adviser for Modern Languages for the Isle of Wight.

Terry Atkinson is a Lecturer in Education and Modern Languages at the University of Bristol School of Education.

In general, the schools where the case studies were observed have not been identified in order to preserve their anonymity.

Acknowledgements

Thanks must be offered to all those pupils and teachers whose work makes up the substance of this book, the case studies in chapter 4. Those contributing case studies include Pam Haezewindt, Carol Macdonald, John Cummings, Robin Page, Christine Eames, David Dyer, Alison Sonnex, Linda Button, Dominic Jones, Michèle Deane, Lucy Atkinson, Mr Gill, John Maxwell and Harbans Jassell. Particular thanks are due to Christine Quantrell for her illuminating chapter on planning for IT, to Mary Ryan for her foreword and for her support and encouragement, to Michèle Deane for the sections on the concept keyboard and databases and for her advice throughout the planning, preparation and compilation of the book and to Peter Boaks, Eric Brown and Ute Hitchin of CILT for their advice, support and encouragement. Thanks are also due to colleagues in the University of Bristol School of Education, in particular, Moira Atkinson and Malcom Lewis for their support and to the PGCE students at Bristol for trialling many of the tasks in the appendices.

Special thanks are due above all to Roger Blamire of NCET for his support to all those working with IT and modern languages. Much of the current good practice in schools, described in the various IT examples in the National Curriculum and catalogued in this book and other publications stems from his influential thinking, the courses he has run and the projects he has supported with NCET funding. Thanks also to Roger and Eric Brown for the preface.

Chapter 1
IT and modern languages the challenge

⚔ Why is IT in the National Curriculum?

NATIONAL CURRICULUM

There are strong economic and cultural arguments for developing the information technology (IT) skills of the nation's school children. The domination of the work place by the microchip, as much in the factory as the office, is a reality that it would be unwise to ignore in the education offered to students. Equally, the role of computers in our culture is growing rapidly and becoming the new literacy. Are you 'computerate' or 'computer literate' is increasingly asked and many of the present generation of teachers have felt marginalised by not being 'in' on computer culture. All pupils deserve the opportunity to become 'computerate'. Furthermore, the full implementation of the National Curriculum will not be accomplished, in the case of modern languages, until the late 1990s. If IT is important now it will be all the more so by then and it is as well that this has been anticipated.

The final report of the National Curriculum Modern Foreign Languages Working Group (DES / WO(2)) devotes considerable space to the ways in which IT can enhance language learning and these are expanded on later in this chapter. IT is ultimately about the storage, retrieval, transmission, processing and presentation of information, much of which is in linguistic form. As such, IT represents a new medium for language and access to it for language learners is crucial, particularly since the information may not be accessible via any other medium.

References to the National Curriculum in this publication are to the National Curriculum in England and Wales.

1

What does the National Curriculum require?

The National Curriculum is a many-headed monster and the answer to the question above is complicated by the fact that there are separate sets of requirements which affect modern languages. These are the Technology Orders and the Modern Foreign Languages (MFL) Order and the Non-Statutory Guidance for each.

The Technology Orders

The Technology Orders were enacted before the MFL Order and apply to all four key stages whereas the latter applies only to key stages 3 and 4. Attainment target 5 of the Technology Orders deals with information technology; its principal focus is to ensure continuity and progression in IT skills. The relevance to modern languages comes from the fact that there is no specific curriculum slot set aside for IT and the attainment targets and programmes of study must be delivered and assessed across all curricular areas. The Technology Orders are statutory and so all schools in England and Wales will have to draw up a whole school policy on IT. Forward-looking schools are already co-ordinating their IT policies in order to see which curricular area can best deliver which aspects of the programmes of study: *'We're to do databases in year 9'*, a head of modern languages recently informed me and it may emerge as a typical pattern that the various types of IT application are shuffled around the departments in this way. A survey of what the various departments in one particular school covered in terms of IT applications by a student teacher on teaching practice concluded that no account had been taken of what other departments were using. From what we know of learning, this would seem counter-productive as it tends to lead to such problems as:

- conflicting messages;
- lack of continuity;
- failure to develop learning transfer;
- lack of consolidation;
- confusion of practical IT skills and procedures.

This lack of co-ordination contributes to the bewilderment of the learners. Equally, the monitoring of progress and recording of attainment in IT skills is not possible without a whole school approach. It is for these reasons that IT has been identified as one of the National Curriculum's cross-curricular skills with the aim of encouraging the development of whole school policies which will help to ensure continuity and progression. Excellent advice on forming a whole school policy on IT is contained in the *Non-Statutory Guidance for IT* (NCC 1990) (see figure 1) and in *Focus on IT* (NCET 1991).

The drawback of all this is that it tends to impose the requirements of a very different curricular area on the modern languages department. Currently, many teachers of modern languages are

APPENDIX 3: IT RESPONSIBILITY OF STAFF IN SECONDARY SCHOOLS

ALL HEADS OF DEPARTMENT

Heads of Department are responsible for ensuring that their departments' schemes of work provide for the use of IT.

Curriculum
*   for National Curriculum subjects, taking account of the IT requirements of programmes of study and statements of attainment;
*   using IT to enhance teaching;
*   identifying components of IT capability which can be developed in the department.

Co-ordination
*   contributing to the IT policy;
*   liaising with the IT co-ordinator to ensure that the department's schemes of work support the school's IT policy.

Resources
*   identifying hardware and software, and how it is to be used.

Staff development and support
*   identifying staff needs for IT INSET;
*   enabling staff to exchange ideas for using IT - through staff workshops, team teaching, sharing worksheets/resources.

Monitoring & review
*   involving all staff in the department in reviewing the use of IT;
*   liaising with the IT co-ordinator to determine where IT is to be assessed.

The following questions may be helpful:
*   How does IT influence teaching in your school/department?
*   Does your scheme of work provide progression and rigour in IT capability?
*   Is the department making the best use of IT resources?

THE TEACHER

The teacher is responsible for the child's IT experiences:
*   using IT to enhance learning;
*   developing each pupil's IT capability in accordance with school policy;
*   ensuring that each pupil has access to IT resources;
*   monitoring and evaluating pupil's experience;
*   determining the next stage in each pupil's use of IT, and ensuring continuity and rigour;
*   contributing to the overall record of development for each child.

Figure 1.1   Reproduced from the Non-Statutory Guidance for IT capability (NCC)

3

enthusiastically developing good practice in the use of concept keyboards, but under a whole school policy they may well be told that concept keyboard applications were covered in key stages 1 and 2 and that they must prioritise on other applications to fit in with the technology orders. This conflict of interest is apparent in the Modern Languages National Curriculum documentation. For example, if we examine some of the IT examples for the higher levels of attainment we often find elementary IT skills. In other cases, there is a good degree of correspondence (e.g. MFL 3.8a and Technology 5.7d both involve selecting a database). The non-statutory guidance for modern languages contains a chart which correlates attainment targets in modern languages and technology (NCC). Policies aimed at harmonising the use of IT on a school-wide basis should be beneficial to modern languages teachers. Once a whole school policy has been devised, teachers should be able to select from a variety of IT packages with which their students are familiar, having covered them in previous years and in other areas of the curriculum. The school policy may also provide opportunities to introduce students to new IT applications as part and parcel of modern languages lessons.

The Modern Foreign Languages Order

The MFL Order stops short of imposing a statutory requirement for IT in modern languages, accepting the advice of the working group, given in its final report:

> 'On resource grounds we are not recommending their [IT examples] immediate inclusion in the modern languages curriculum'. (17.22)

Modern languages may have followed in the footsteps of English but it is difficult to square this reluctance with the statutory requirement contained in the Technology Orders to deliver IT across the curriculum. Nevertheless, there is a strong advocacy for IT. For example, in the general requirements for the programmes of study we read (DES/HMSO 1991):

> 'All pupils should have opportunities in both key stages to develop information technology capability through the programmes of study.' (P.21.)

4

To back this requirement there are a number of specific references to IT in the examples illustrating the statements of attainment. There are three given for AT4 (writing), five in AT3 (reading) and two in AT1 (listening).

NB. no examples are included in AT2 (speaking) as a result of the policy of omitting any reference to the stimulus for speaking.

In addition to these explicit references to IT the Order offers many opportunities for the use of IT. The programmes of study include various activities which could imply the use of IT, for example:

> • *produce a variety of types of writing*
> • *redraft their own writing to improve its accuracy and presentation*
> • *redraft an existing written text (including their own) for a different audience or purpose*
> • *record and express information in different forms (eg text, tables, charts, graphs), for different audiences*
> • *conduct surveys and other investigations in the class, school or outside*
> • *use the target language in a real or simulated adult environment*
> • *work independently of the teacher'* (pp.23-26).

All of these activities can be greatly facilitated if IT is available and if teachers and pupils have the necessary skills.

Software

When computers first became available in schools, they were often seen as a potential ally in carrying out the routine aspects of language teaching such as grammar drilling. Early examples of software included verb testing programs, vocabulary quizzes, gap-filling exercises and multiple choice tests. These were sometimes presented in the format of games which it was felt would motivate learners through otherwise boring but necessary learning. Known collectively as Computer Assisted Language Learning (CALL), this type of approach is prevalent in higher education.

Others saw this approach as fundamentally opposed to the move towards communicative language teaching and a more learner-centred approach. Barry Jones, in particular, developed software such as *Quelle tête* (CUP) and *Granville* (CUP) which were more attuned to emerging good practice. Though quite different from earlier CALL programs, the approach was still very much subject specific.

Latterly, a move towards greater authenticity in IT has sprung up. This requires the use of generic IT packages as found in the real world, for example word processing in offices, data-bases in travel agencies, stock control programs in shops and viewdata systems

5

Three types of software

(teletext) in the home. Examples of these different approaches to IT are present in the final report but, as Blamire (1991) points out, it is possible to discern in that report:

'a shift ... to more flexible and open-ended generic IT tools (word processing and data handling software) with which pupils will be increasingly familiar and which they will use in their working lives.' (P. 48)

Jenkins and Servel-Way (1991) also foresee the use of more authentic IT applications as a logical consequence of the type of IT advocated in the modern languages final report, arguing that:

'Modern linguists must realise that the majority of existing CAL packages, however useful they may be in the classroom, will do little to contribute towards the delivery of (MFL) attainment target 4' (P.58)

Whilst of course no-one will be forced to abandon software they have come to rely on, they will have to consider whether they are using a wide enough range of IT applications. The need to meet the technology orders for IT across the curriculum also implies the use of generic software.

How can this book help with IT planning?

If you've read this far it should already have helped to clarify the basic issues. Elsewhere in the handbook you will find sections which cover the following matters as practically as possible within the confines of the printed page:

curriculum planning an approach to IT planning and the National Curriculum is set out in Chapter 2;

software what is available; what a minimum requirement might be given the requirements of the National Curriculum; what most schools currently use;

hardware what the options are; what modern languages departments can reasonably demand; how to make the most of limited resources;

good practice in the case studies you will find examples of how teachers are already implementing the requirements of the National Curriculum;

IT tasks and skills the appendices describe some of the basic IT skills modern languages teachers require.

How can IT enhance language learning?

As mentioned earlier, this is addressed in some detail in section 8.35 of the final report (DES / WO(2)) of the working group. Possibly the most important point is that IT can enhance language learning but can also contribute to the overall development of the student through:

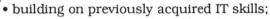

- building on previously acquired IT skills;
- providing a worthwhile and realistic experience that meets immediate needs as well as long-term ones;
- increasing the interaction with other students and thereby developing social and communication skills.

These other elements need to be borne in mind in assessing the value of IT in language learning.

Authenticity

Authentic work-related tasks using IT can easily be simulated in modern languages classrooms or in a computer network room. There are various examples among the case studies and Wood's *1992 Experience* (St. Martin's College) is a prime example. Because the computer is such a common tool in the work place, it does not require a great deal of imagination to set up a work-related task - particularly if generic IT applications are available. In this area the requirements of the technology orders converge with TVEI-inspired thinking about teaching and learning styles. Learners can be motivated by working on tasks which are clearly recognised as adult activities. From a linguistic point of view, these tasks provide a context for language use and many opportunities for spontaneity.

Authenticity of material is another aspect of IT. An obvious example is *Minitel*, the French telephone information service which has virtually replaced the telephone directory. This important language-based source of information is only accessible via a modem, a computer and special software. *Minitel* provides constantly up-dated on-line information on a very wide range of topics. Increasingly, information of many kinds will be either exclusively available through electronic storage and retrieval, or else the alternatives will be so much more cumbersome as to render them near useless.

Autonomy

Through the use of IT we can create a self-contained learning resource which offers students as much or as little support as they require. Such a fully differentiated learning environment empowers learners to direct their own learning. With just one computer, a modern languages classroom can be set up to allow individuals or small groups to work autonomously within a flexible system of classroom management. The MFL Order recognises the key role of IT in developing the ability to learn independently and lists the use of computers as one of four key ways of promoting learner autonomy (p.26).

Cross-curricular skills

The National Curriculum Council (NCC 1990) defines six basic cross-curricular skills, amongst which it includes IT. As mentioned earlier, the way in which we use IT in modern languages can become part of a coherent whole school policy which takes account of work in preceding key stages. In this way, modern languages can harness skills the pupils already have, consolidate these skills and develop them. This promotes continuity in the learner's experience of education which is vital if he or she is to interpret that experience meaningfully; without this continuity progress can be seriously curtailed. In modern languages, where so much is new and alien to the learner, a continuity of experience is all the more important. A cross-curricular approach to IT is akin to a language across the curriculum policy, where the main emphasis is on a harmonised approach rather than on team teaching across departments. Of course, opportunities to work collaboratively with other departments are possible and these can help to cement whole school policies. For example, in one school a joint project between modern languages and art has been established to write, illustrate and publish foreign language readers. With geography, history, English and science it is possible to set up joint projects with link schools abroad using electronic mail, databases and so forth.

Access

Access to IT provision is a thorny question and the final report has platitudes to offer which are unlikely to yield results. The working group call for an:

> 'investment and development programme of IT in modern language classrooms and learning schemes.' (17.24)

It is difficult not to be pessimistic about the chances of this becoming reality given the long history of underfunding in the public sector of education and the high cost of satisfactorily equipping all subject areas in all schools. In view of the problem of restricted access, the need for careful planning in how to use the scarce IT resource most effectively and in such a way as to meet the statutory requirements of the National Curriculum is all the more important.

The question of access also relates to learners with special educational needs. For some of these students IT may, for reasons of physical or sensory disability or due to learning difficulties, provide the only means of access to the curriculum. This is particularly true of Attainment Target 4, where many learners can be enabled to produce writing which matches their intellectual development, as evidenced in their reading ability, by using IT. Many teachers of modern languages are concerned about the provision of modern languages for all learners in the 11-16 age range, particularly with a rigorously prescribed curriculum. Whilst IT is not a panacea, it does have the power to enable the least able to achieve worthwhile results in writing which would not be possible by other means. The particular role of IT in supporting the language learning of children with special educa-

8

tional needs has been specifically addressed in *'Languages for All'* (NCET 1991). As this booklet amply indicates, a large proportion of the initiatives to start teaching modern languages to children in special schools have a strong IT component. If we think of the inspirational writer Christy Brown, subject of the film *My left foot*, we can comprehend the power of IT to unlock the potential of some learners.

As discussed earlier, IT can provide access for all language learners to information not otherwise available, for example via the *Minitel* system in France. Few could deny the special place of cassette recorders in modern languages and a similar case is beginning to be made for video and satellite TV. IT is rapidly assuming a high priority in the eyes of many modern languages teachers for largely similar reasons - because it can bring the sounds, words and images of the foreign language, embedded in their culture, into the classroom.

Motivation

Learners using IT are frequently observed to show increased motivation and enthusiasm for language learning. The reasons for this vary according to the type of work and the particular learners involved but can be listed as follows:

- IT is a more practical way of working;
- IT can enhance the status of language through high quality print-out and VDU display, for example the status of Asian languages can be enhanced when the facility to word process is available;
- using the computer allows the learner to work more independently from the teacher and any errors are private;
- a well-structured and differentiated task can lead to positive reinforcement if the student is able to achieve more than by conventional methods (for example, using a database, some quite complex search routines can be managed);
- the learner can work at his or her own pace, the computer never tires of the wrong answer.

Stimulation

When using the computer, learners may be stimulated to attempt much more than they otherwise would. Teachers have observed pupils who have shown little or no spirit of adventure in conventional lessons suddenly come alive with an IT activity. Equally, learners using word processing packages have been observed to write much more and with greater imagination than when writing by hand (Atkinson forthcoming).

Collaboration

Pupils are able to work together when using the computer in ways which enhance their learning, their achievement and their social skills. When using a text manipulation package such as *Fun with texts* (Camsoft) they will share insight into the structure of the text, when writing collaboratively they will pool ideas. This collaboration will often involve other members of the class. The prominence of the VDU and the neutrality (no ink blots) of the display mean that students are much more open to the idea of looking at each others' work. In a network room ideas can spread around a class like wildfire. This often generates a lot of reading of each others' work and some teachers have capitalised on this natural curiosity by building it into tasks. Teachers may also join in with this process of collaboration and be seen less in the role of an adjudicator of linguistic accuracy. They are able to assist pupils in their ongoing work without leaving a tell-tale trail of red ink.

There are a variety of ways in which IT can enhance language learning and yet many language teachers are still unsure if they have the necessary skills to 'do' IT.

Can I 'do' IT?

It is possible to build up a defensive barrier due to a lack of confidence and fear of ridicule by the computer whizz-kids in year 8. This can lead to a real phobia, which must be taken seriously. To help overcome such a phobia, there needs to be a clear understanding of the importance and value of IT. There is a need for sensible and sensitive in-service training. It should then be possible to adopt the healthy attitude taken by many colleagues, whose line to pupils runs:

'I know you understand these computers much better than I do, so please help me out if anything goes wrong.'

Such phobics also need the time to sit down on their own and build up their confidence by working through simple IT tasks, such as those contained in appendix 1 and appendix 2. But it is not merely a question of the teachers concerned making all the adjustments; software designers and computer manufacturers must also improve the quality of their products so that they are more user-friendly, more compatible and more intuitive to use. There is more than a grain of truth in the current TV advertisement for a leading make of computer in which one executive replies to another:

'You haven't got the wrong people, you've got the wrong computers.'

Of course, technical back-up and support should be available from an IT co-ordinator / network manager based in the school and from advisory teachers with expertise in modern languages IT applications.

Another aspect of the resistance to using IT is fear and resentment of change. Many teachers have worked long and hard to establish their existing practices and are naturally loath to change them. The incorporation of IT into schemes of work would clearly necessitate such revision. There are also those wary of yet another false technological dawn, remembering the way in which the language laboratory and the audio-visual approach were greeted enthusiastically, only to be subsequently discredited and abandoned. The bewildering pace of innovation within the computer world itself does little to allay such fears. The case for IT has been made earlier in this chapter and elsewhere, more eloquently, by many others. It is, in this writer's view, overwhelming. The change required to integrate IT is a necessary change rather than change

11

for its own sake. More fundamentally, it is doubtless as wrong to stick unbendingly to established practices as it is to jump on every new bandwagon. As the modern languages teaching force ages there is a danger of stagnation. It is important that we continue to show the same spirit of innovation that has transformed modern languages and prepared it for the central role it is now to play in the National Curriculum as one of the foundation subjects. A willingness to integrate IT into the scheme of work is surely worthwhile.

Summary

The National Curriculum in England and Wales will not be fully implemented until almost the end of the century. By that time, the level of IT resourcing may or may not have improved significantly. However, an approach to IT based on careful planning and integration into schemes of work should ensure that the use made of IT does improve. In the next chapter it will be argued that the source of good IT practice is usually teachers who have developed good modern languages practice rather than technical 'experts'. The case studies in Chapter 3 are examples of good (perhaps 'interesting' is a better word) practice by modern languages teachers. These case studies are intended to provide ideas that other teachers can adapt and develop. In researching these case studies a great deal of excellent work was uncovered. The National Curriculum will provide the spur to disseminate this and to take a coherent approach to the planning and integration of IT in both modern languages schemes of work and whole school policies.

References

Atkinson T A, 'Le hamster a mangé mon pneu : creative writing and IT', *Language Learning Journal*, (forthcoming).
Blamire R, 'Computers can speak volumes', *Times Educational Supplement* , (15 III 1991).
DES, *National Curriculum: draft order for modern foreign languages*, DES (11 VII 1991).
DES / WO(1), *National Curriculum modern foreign languages working group initial advice* , DES 1990.
DES / WO(2) , *National Curriculum: modern foreign languages for ages 11 to 16 : proposals of the Secretary of State for Education and Science and the Secretary of State for Wales*, HMSO 1990.
DES / WO(3), *Technology in the National Curriculum*, HMSO (1990).

DES / WO(4), *Modern foreign languages in the National Curriculum*, HMSO (1991).

Jenkins S A & M Servel-Way, 'The national curriculum in modern languages: delivering IT', *Language Learning Journal*, No.3 (1991).

NCC(1), *The National Curriculum Council consultation report : modern foreign languages*, NCC (1991).

NCC(2), *Curriculum guidance no 3 : the whole curriculum* , NCC (1990).

NCC(3), *Non-statutory guidance: information technology capability* NCC (1990).

NCC(4), *Non-statutory guidance: modern foreign languages*, NCC (1992).

NCET(1), *Focus on IT* , NCET (1991).

NCET(2), *Languages for All* , NCET (1991).

Further reading

Hewer S, *Making the most of IT skills*, CILT (1989, 1992).

Rendall H, *Making the most of micro-computers*, CILT (1991).

NCET, *Learning Languages with Technology*, NCET (1988).

Chapter 2
Planning for IT

The purpose of this chapter is to examine some of the issues that need to be addressed when planning for the use of information technology in the modern languages classroom within the framework of the National Curriculum. The chapter is concerned with the issues which relate particularly to long-term planning within a scheme of work but begins by trying to define a rationale which applies also to the planning of lessons and smaller units of work. As such the chapter may be helpful to heads of department in planning the modern languages element of the curriculum but could equally be of use to teachers thinking about the use of IT within individual lessons. The chapter aims to be as practical and realistic as possible and has been written for modern linguists rather than technical experts. Further help can be found in the Non-Statutory Guidance for Modern Foreign Languages (NCC).

Not all pupils are naturally enthusiastic about the use of technology!

In the current climate of change the number of aspects of teaching and learning that the individual teacher has to address is enormous and all are overshadowed by questions about the form, duration, content (or not!) of assessment. It is entirely reasonable that in such a climate IT should appear near the bottom of the list of priorities for all but the technically enthusiastic. This chapter starts with the premise that, however interesting and rewarding the use of information technology may be for its own sake, it is not the first priority for most teachers of modern languages. Then again, not all teachers (or indeed, contrary to popular opinion, all pupils) are naturally enthusiastic about the use of technology. The temptation then is to leave the planning for IT within the area of modern languages to the IT enthusiast. It is the basic argument of this chapter that this is a mistake and that teachers of modern languages need to use their expertise to decide appropriate uses of technology within the learning of a foreign language. It is the contention of this chapter that the most effective planning will be done by those who are most enthusiastic about teaching and learning languages and who assimilate and integrate the use of IT within good modern language practice.

Resourcing

It may be helpful to begin, where many teachers begin, with the question of resourcing. (This will be taken up again in more detail later.) The wide range of information processing technology currently available is exciting, but the enormous variety and the pace of change is daunting even for an enthusiastic languages teacher. There is also no doubt that the same variety has in the past encouraged schools and departments to make expensive mistakes. The typical modern languages department often struggles to replace old audio equipment and cannot afford such mistakes. For this reason, and also because of the ingrained suspicion of all things technical which seems to have been fostered in languages departments by reel-to-reel tapes and ancient slide projectors, the modern languages teacher tends to approach IT cautiously, if at all. This caution, if properly directed, can be of benefit because it gives time to think and to ask questions. As all teachers know to their cost, labels can be misleading. GCSE in bold letters on the front cover may have sold books but did not disguise courses written with different criteria in mind. There is nothing intrinsically good (or bad) about information technology. It is in selecting and using software or hardware in particular classrooms with particular children for a defined purpose that we can measure its worth. Departments' needs are different, their objectives and their teaching styles and their resources are different and, whilst there are cross-curricular similarities and applications within schools, thought also should be given to the particular needs of the modern languages department and to the most suitable and flexible IT applications to deliver the aims and objectives of that department.

Planning for the use of IT, as with the use of any method or item of equipment, needs to be approached in a balanced way. We need to accept that:

- there are times and situations where there are good reasons for not using IT;

- there are some items of hardware and software which are of poor quality;

- there are some items of hardware and software which are not suitable for the particular school we teach in;

- there are some items of hardware and software which, however good and suitable they may be, are not within the budget of the department.

We need then to select with care what we buy, but what criteria do we use and how does this relate to planning for use with classes? In order to plan and buy effectively we need to examine our reasons for using IT in the first place. These may be many and varied.

'To amuse the 3rd years on Friday afternoon.'

'As a treat for the pupils who finish their real work first.'

'To teach the first years adjectival endings.'

'Because I like fiddling about with computers.'

'Because the National Curriculum says I'm supposed to.'

Whatever our reasons for using IT we need to have an underlying rationale for its use or we are wasting our own and our pupils' time. In fact, it is debatable whether there is any point in using IT in schools unless it is integrated into the curriculum and subjected to the same scrutiny as the use of chalk and the blackboard. However valid the reasons for using IT in school and however many arguments there are to justify IT for its own sake, to a busy modern languages teacher it only really becomes a priority when it can be seen to support language learning. In other words, when the use of IT as one resource amongst others helps to deliver objectives in terms of language learning. In the context of the National Curriculum when there are so many new demands facing the language teacher, the real justification for the use of IT lies in its ability to help languages teachers to deliver some of these new demands. It is from this perspective that we can begin to develop a rationale for the use of IT which belongs in, and is part of the modern languages classroom.

To summarise then, the points made so far are:

- that IT should be used selectively taking into account departmental needs and differences;

- that the best person to plan for its use in the modern languages classroom is the enthusiastic modern linguist;

- as with all resources, balance and a healthy sense of perspective are needed;

- real justification for the use of IT is as an integral part of the language curriculum helping to deliver objectives in terms of language learning.

Integrating IT in the modern languages lesson

It is difficult to take a long-term perspective without some appreciation of short-term benefits and implications. Beginning then with the objective of IT as an integrated part of the modern languages classroom let us look first at developing a rationale for the use of IT within individual lessons. As is indicated in other chapters, information technology is more than just computers, but to simplify matters I will use computers as an example of possibilities in this section.

In planning work on the computer the following questions are intended as a starting point to think through objectives. The same questions can be useful in evaluating the role a computer is playing within an individual lesson.

1. What is the purpose of the computer task?

2. How does it fit into the pattern of the work being done?

3. Could the task on the computer be done effectively using other resources?

4. Is the computer distracting attention from the other language activities or is it supporting / extending them?

1. What is the purpose of the computer task?

It is easy to fall into the trap of using the computer as a stop gap, a time filler or a reward. We need to think about what purpose the computer task is serving and how this relates to our objectives for the lesson. If the target area of vocabulary in a particular lesson is weather, then it makes little sense for the computer task to involve shopping (unless this is part of some longer-term plan).

The computer can be an effective way of learning vocabulary and the pupils may leave the lesson thinking that the subject was shopping and not weather!

It is also very easy to adopt methods which we would otherwise be very unhappy about using, just because there is a piece of software in the department which allows us to use the computer in a particular lesson. We need to be clear about what we are using the computer to achieve and make sure that it fits our objectives for the lesson on a number of levels:

- that it is introducing, reinforcing or extending the area of language involved in the rest of the classwork;

- that the methodology involved in the computer task is consistent with methods we would normally employ in the classroom;

- that the task encourages better understanding, manipulation or use of language.

2. How does it fit into the pattern of the work being done?

Having considered the appropriacy of the use of the computer in terms of language objectives, we need to think about organisation or classroom management. It is more difficult to integrate work when the class migrates once a fortnight to the computer room. If this is the case, then longer-term plans need to tie the computer sessions into previous and subsequent language work. The regular presence of one or two computers in the classroom makes integration easier but means that the computer task must be organised to fit into the pattern of the rest of the work.

There is no doubt that the use of information technology forces teachers to look at classroom organisation in a different way. It is difficult to sustain a totally teacher-directed approach and use information technology in the classroom. The alternatives are many and varied and depend upon the objectives of the lesson, the number of pupils and computers and how many different activities the teacher feels able to cope with at once. The following are some examples beginning with organisationally simpler alternatives.

a) Pupils complete individual work (for example follow a reading scheme or continue with classwork set by the teacher) and groups of three pupils at a time complete a text manipulation exercise on the computer using part of the reading scheme or a previously introduced text. The length of the computer task would need to be designed so that all pupils were able to complete the task in one or two lessons on a rota. Again, the computer task would need to be designed to reflect the kind of work being completed in the rest of the lesson.

b) Pupils may do pair-work, for example oral work based upon dialogues. The computer task could reflect this by asking pupils to re-order a similar dialogue in response to a tape recording. (Dual headphones attached to a walkman allow pairs to work at the computer with a tape recording.) Again the length of the task would be important and a rota (formal or informal) would be needed.

(In the previous examples the teacher is basically managing two different activities. More complex to organise are variations of group work where the tasks are all linked and form common objectives or lead to a product when all the tasks are completed.)

c) The objective may be as simple as learning to use a particular set of structures, for example, in the café. Different tasks involving the computer, the tape recorder, oral work, reading comprehension, etc would be designed around this central objective.

d) At a different level, each of the tasks might give pupils part of a puzzle and by working through them they put all the information together and solve the puzzle. Tasks prepared for this kind of work must be able to be done in any order and timing is important. There should also be a mixture of tasks, some of which pupils can do without any teacher assistance.

e) The traditional circus where groups move around the room as they finish each task can be useful in creating a sense of pace and organisation but has several disadvantages.

- all tasks must take the same amount of time;

- groups need to be roughly the same size where equipment is involved (easier when there are two computers and groups of six can be split into two groups of three when they arrive at the computer task);

- some individuals will always finish ahead of others and it is more difficult to cater for them in this arrangement;

- slower pupils may feel under pressure and may leave many tasks incomplete.

f) Another alternative is to have a central core of tasks which pupils complete in groups at their own tables, moving only to use, for example, the tape recorder or the computer. In general this means that sufficient resources for the main tasks need to be available for most of the pupils most of the time (or the teacher must restrict group or individual choices). Pupils also need to be helped to organise their work. The advantages are that:

- individuals can progress at their own pace;
- not all pupils are changing task at the same time;
- demand for help from the teacher with initial instructions is spread more evenly through the lesson.

19

f) In the final example the computer is used to create or support a particular kind of classroom organisation. This may be done by using a computerised simulation which also involves other non-computer based tasks (one example of this is *Granville*), or it may be done by using various sources of information (audio and videotapes, brochures, leaflets, letters, etc) of which the computer is just one more. A simple database containing information from the tourist information office, a hotel, a lost property office or a train station can be used to create lots of different tasks.

3. Could the task on the computer be done effectively using other resources?

If the answer is yes it is usually easier to use other resources and to use the computer for relevant tasks which cannot be done in other ways. This is especially true when it takes a lot of effort to get the computer into the classroom in the first place!

4. Is the computer distracting attention from the other language activities or is it supporting/extending them?

This brings us back to the earlier point about the computer as a source of motivation. If the computer activity is used as a separate item, a reward or a distraction, the source of motivation may draw attention away from the language work encouraging pupils to scramble through the real work so that they can play on the computer. Where the computer is an integrated part of the classroom it is possible to use that motivation to support or

Pupils can be encouraged to collect all the information to find the deliberate mistakes

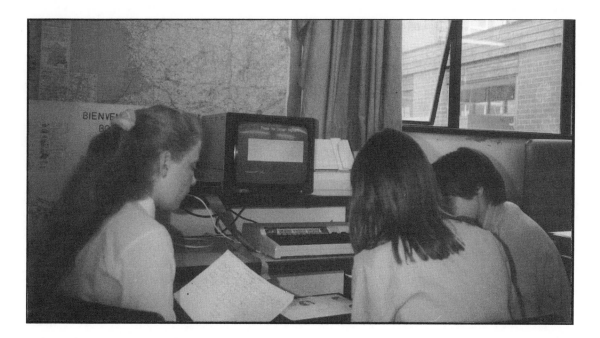

extend the other language activities. This is especially true when information is shared between the tasks. For example, if pupils have to listen carefully to a tape recording in order to get the information they need to compare with the computer-based information, then it may be more motivating than a listening task which is complete in itself. This is one way of using the computer to add realism or purpose to language activities instead of a way to occupy spare time at the end of the lesson.

Not all work of this kind needs to be complicated, nor is it limited to transactional language situations. A simple example could be built around descriptions of members of a family. Different parts o˙ the description may be given on a tape recording, text illustr₂ted with pictures and a simple database. By making two or thrₑe pieces of information contradictory, pupils can be encouraged ₜo collect all the information to find the deliberate mistakes.

Summary

Planning for the use of IT within lessons or small units of work involves thinking clearly about its purpose in relation to the objectives we have set. This is not just in relation to language learning itself, but will involve thinking about the amount of independence we want the learners to exercise and the pattern of classroom organisation that we want to use. Obviously, the pattern will vary according to the objectives we have set and the pupils involved. Variety is important, but in the long term we may need to think about the implications for learner independence and construct organisational objectives as well as strictly linguistic objectives. Integrating IT so that it gives purpose and adds an extra dimension to language work may, initially, involve more thought but makes more sense than using a potentially powerful motivator to distract attention from the real objectives of the lesson.

Integrating IT - a long-term perspective

So far we have considered some of the issues involved in using the computer as an integrated part of a lesson and examined some of the ways in which the computer might make an impact upon the modern languages classroom. In long-term planning within the context of the National Curriculum there are, however, other issues to be considered. How seriously should the head of a modern languages department consider long-term planning for IT given that there are so many other time-consuming aspects of the implementation of the National Curriculum?

One response is to underline the many ways in the consultation reports in which the use of information technology is taken as an integral part of language learning. In the draft documents IT was referred to within many different sections and the following are some examples:

1. Recommendations in various chapters of the final Report of the National Curriculum MFL Working Group

    a) Introduction

> *'Audio, video and information technology all open up a range of new possibilities for communicative activities such as accessing reference data, using word processors to re-draft text and analyse language, and communicating via international electronic mail boxes with schools in other countries.' (p.4, 3.9)*

    b) References to use in special educational needs

> *'The use of information technology to support modern foreign language teaching is particularly helpful to pupils with special educational needs.' (p.77, 13.11)*

    c) References to cross-curricular opportunities

> *'The NCC identifies six basic areas of skill.....*
> *iv) Information Technology.'*

    d) References within attainment targets

> *'Some of our examples suggest the use of information technology. We do not mean to imply that these are the only circumstances where IT could be used, and we would wish to encourage its use wherever appropriate.'*

e) References to programmes of study

> *'Learners require frequent opportunities to ...
> use computers (if available) for purposes such
> as problem-solving games, information-retrieval,
> word-processing, desk-top publishing and
> electronic mail contacts.'*

f) References to good practice

Examples given in 10.12 (p.60)   10.19 (p.62)   10.22 (p.62)

g) Resource implications

1. Initial teacher training.

> *'...a programme to ensure all modern languages
> students are enabled to maximise classroom
> deployment of appropriate forms of information
> technology.' (p.89, 17.4)*

2. In-service training.

> *'...the integration of information technology...'
> (p.90, 17.3)*

3. Classroom resources

> *'With the development of modern languages as
> an increasingly practical discipline the time has
> come for an appropriate level of investment in
> the technology to service the needs of a modern
> curriculum.' (p.92, 17.23)*

The implications are summarised in the final consultation report
(NCC 1991):

> 'All pupils should have opportunities in both
> key stages to develop information technology
> capability through the programmes of study.'
> (p.38)

This response, whilst painting a background picture, is not
particularly helpful in approaching the practical task of long-term
planning nor perhaps in deciding priorities. Just as in planning
a single lesson involving IT we turned first to linguistic objectives
and good modern language practice to decide the role and place
of the computer, it is helpful and sensible to use the same
guidelines in long-term planning. The question then is, what
particular aspects of language learning are we trying to address
within a scheme of work. The following list of aspects given in the
final report (DES/WO 1991) is a useful summary and a good place
to start:

*'Teachers will need to reappraise the planning
and execution of their lessons and their use of
available resources, and to develop appropriate
teaching strategies in the light of the following ...*

- *the nature of progression in modern
  languages learning and its implications for
  teaching approaches;*

- *teaching languages to the full ability range
  with special reference to pupils at both ends
  of the range;*

- *clearer differentiation within the modern
  languages classroom;*

- *the development of greater independence for
  the learner through flexible learning
  techniques;*

- *use of the target language in the classroom
  by teacher and pupil;*

- *the management and exploitation of a
  variety of resources and media in the
  classroom;*

- *the integration of information technology;*

- *new approaches to assessment including
  where appropriate peer and self-
  assessment;*

- *the treatment of cross-curricular themes in
  modern languages, in particular through
  collaboration with other departments;' (p.90
  17.13).*

If these are taken as objectives in overall planning, then the
integration of information technology is just one item in a list. If,
however, we look at the other items in the list and see how an
integrated use of IT can help to deliver these, the perspective
changes. Let us take a number of these items separately and look
at the possibilities.

**Progression /
differentiation**

Progression on an individual basis, as opposed to a class pro-
gramme, leads to the problem of differentiation in the classroom.
The use of IT can help to provide differentiation in both task and
outcome in very simple ways. For example, the use of a text
manipulation package with a text which forms part of the overall
lesson, can enable the individual pupil to progress in easy steps
from comprehension of the broad pattern of the text (re-ordering

Using the computer as one resource amongst many

the lines) to supported reproduction (cloze). The teacher provides differentiation by encouraging pupils at different stages to attack the same text in different ways. Or where form filling may be a pen and paper exercise, support with a matching program can open the exercise to those who need initial support.

The full ability range

Catering for special needs at both ends of the ability range can be made easier by using IT. For example, the use of a word bank and the concept keyboard is one way of enabling pupils to create imaginative written work with varying degrees of support. The same technique can be used with able pupils beginning a new area of vocabulary and structures or by providing them with more complex structures and requiring them to use the word processor for basic structures. Or again the same word bank can be used with different tasks. A simple description and a summary of a longer piece of writing may require the same area of vocabulary and structures but the tasks differ in complexity.

Independence / variety of resources

One of the main difficulties in developing greater independence in the communicative language classroom, particularly in the beginning stages, is the fact that the teacher is seen as the only source of the language. Using the computer as one resource amongst many enables the pupils to work with support, but without direct teacher support. In the beginning this may be for very short periods of time, but with the right choice of software pupils can work individually, in pairs or in groups from the first stages of learning a language. When authoring packages are used, the teacher can tailor this to the needs of the class so that the content is meaningful and the level is appropriate. The use of databases in conjunction with cassette tapes, videos, brochures, etc can help to create realistic situations and make connections between the different resources, making classroom management easier.

Target language

If use of the target language is not to be restricted to the teacher, then it is important to create situations in which pupils have real reasons for using the target language. One way is by providing an information gap. This can be done with the computer (on its own or in conjunction with other resources) where some pupils have access to the information on the computer and the others don't. The information and tasks can be made more or less complex, from the price of stamps in the post-office to details of company products.

Another way of encouraging the use of the target language is by allowing a group of pupils to work around the computer to produce a written task. Where typing is slow, again the use of a word bank with the concept keyboard may be useful. Even using a text manipulation package in pairs or threes can produce oral work.

Of course, the pupils may resort to English in any situation where the teacher gives control of the activity over to the pupils. This may be acceptable in text manipulation exercises if the pupils are discussing the form and structure of the foreign language. However, pupils can and will use the target language if:

- the language they need has been systematically presented (e.g. technical terms such as disk and print, the language of negotiation such as *'Shall we insert...?'* ;

- the teacher has high expectations about the use of target language;

- the computer software displays messages and instructions on-screen in the target language.

Cross-curricular themes

The use of IT can itself be a good focus for cross-curricular work (whether by employing the expensive use of electronic mail within an international cross-curricular project or two computers linked within the school during a cross-curricular lesson or day) but also where the language used in other curriculum areas may be too complex for the level within the language classroom, the use of IT can help the modern languages teacher to simplify both the content and the presentation of the work. For example, there are many areas of common interest within history and geography but long scripts in the target language may be too complex. Simplifying texts in text manipulation packages, or sorting and entering information into a database in simpler language may make cross-curricular tasks more accessible for younger language learners.

If we approach the integration of IT from this perspective, it becomes a way of implementing good practice in the language classroom rather than another item to labour over. It becomes a facilitator and a support to language teachers and learners. The questions become more specific. Within the overall scheme, you might ask where can I use IT :

- to support?
- to provide differentiated tasks?
- to build tasks with differentiated outcomes?
- to extend?
- to consolidate?
- to facilitate different learning patterns?
- to create different kinds of classroom management?
- to develop multi-skill work?
- to initiate cross-curricular work?

The answers to these questions do not have to be expensive or complicated. With a small number of authoring packages it is possible to develop a bank of files which can be used across the age and ability range and which respond to these questions.

27

Summary

To summarise, planning for IT in the MFL National Curriculum is all about exploring ways in which IT can support and extend good practice. It should be approached as a possible solution, rather than another problem, to improve modern languages learning.

Making a start

Everyone plans in different ways and it is not intended to offer the perfect planning model, but if you have a limited knowledge of computers, a limited budget and want to begin planning for its use within a scheme of work the following suggestions may be useful.

• Choose a small number of flexible software packages and, if you don't know already, learn how to use them.

• Investigate a few of the authoring packages suggested in this book and, if necessary, try to find someone within the school / LEA who can help you to do this.

• For each of the pieces of software, take each of the questions below and try to think of practical ways in which you might use the software in the classroom:

     * to support?
     * to provide differentiated tasks?
     * to build tasks with differentiated outcomes?
     * to extend?
     * to consolidate?
     * to facilitate different learning patterns / different kinds of classroom management?
     * to develop multi-skill work?
     * to initiate cross-curricular work?

     If this is too difficult without a context, take one of the Areas of Experience and think of specific examples.

• Now that you have some ideas try to be more specific. Choose an area of experience, a key stage and a group of levels within the attainment targets (e.g. 1-3 / 6-7 etc). Read those levels within each of the attainment targets.

     * What sort of help phrases should pupils be able to use at this stage?
     * Which organisational level are they working at?
     * How much unfamiliar vocabulary / structures are pupils expected to deal with?
     * How much support should they have?
     * What kinds of IT are suitable at the levels you have chosen?

Can you use IT...
* to provide help phrases?
* to support suitable forms of classroom organisation?
* to provide support / extension for language skills?

• Once you have some ideas for a small area try them out with specific classes. Then begin to think about progress through a Key Stage. Remember that pupils will make progress in the number of pieces of software they can use as well as their language work and that they will need to develop the appropriate vocabulary in the target language, if you want to integrate the computer work into the language work.

• Be realistic in planning!

Begin with a small number of specific objectives. Keep in mind the resources available and the number of staff who will need to use them when planning for specific uses of IT within the scheme of work. Beginning with one year group, make a small number of computer-based activities a core element of the course during that year and make sure all members of staff who teach the year group have the amount of access they need to the relevant equipment and the support they need to use it in the classroom. This can then be built upon in subsequent years knowing that all classes in that year have had a minimum of experience.

Try to find ways of supporting staff, by spending departmental time looking at a specific software package, by occasional team teaching when trying out new uses in the classroom, by involving other departments / staff in exploring particular uses of IT.

Conclusion

To conclude, planning for the use of IT in modern languages is about the effective integration of an exciting resource into the classroom practice of the modern languages department. The modern linguist should determine its use according to clear objectives and should not be afraid to reject uses of information technology which detract from the central purposes of language learning. There are many very positive benefits in using IT occasionally in the classroom, but to move from ad hoc use by some teachers in some classes to a consistent and progressive use means tackling departmental organisation and planning. This will not happen overnight, but as the modern languages scheme of work becomes the central pivot in the implementation of the National Curriculum, so the place and purpose of IT within that scheme will need to be found and evaluated.

References

DES / WO(1), *National Curriculum modern foreign languages working group initial advice* , DES 1990.

DES / WO(2) , *National Curriculum: modern foreign languages for ages 11 to 16 : proposals of the Secretary of State for Education and Science and the Secretary of State for Wales*, HMSO 1990.

NCC(1), *The National Curriculum Council consultation report : modern foreign languages*, NCC (1991).

NCC(2), *Modern Foreign Languages Non-Statutory Guidance*, NCC (1992).

Chapter 3
Hardware and software

In this chapter the various types of hardware and software available for use in modern languages are described and explained. In order to give a reasonably realistic picture of current practice a survey of modern languages departments was carried out in 1991. A total of 120 responses were received. The charts contained in this chapter are based on this survey. The survey mainly involved teachers in three local education authorities and is therefore affected by local policies such as standardisation on the make of computer within one LEA.

Hardware

The hardware, or computer equipment, available to modern languages teachers varies tremendously between schools in terms of how many computers are available. Figure 3.1 gives an indication of this variation. Teachers were asked to say how many computers there were in their schools to which they had access. Few if any of these computers would be reserved for the exclusive use of modern languages. Interestingly some schools have open access to whole school facilities and others do not. Several teachers wrote comments on their survey forms to the effect that access to such facilities was theoretically possible but rendered difficult in practice by the block time-tabling of computer studies classes.

As well as variation in levels of provision there are several different makes of computer com-

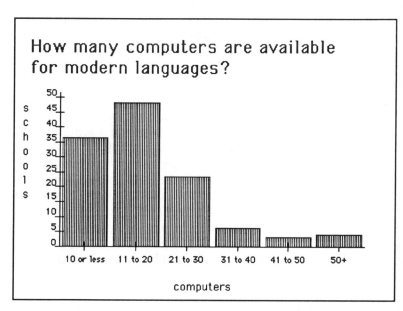

Figure 3.1

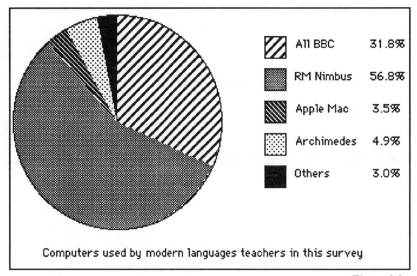

All BBC	31.8%
RM Nimbus	56.8%
Apple Mac	3.5%
Archimedes	4.9%
Others	3.0%

Computers used by modern languages teachers in this survey

Figure 3.2

monly found in schools and for each make a profusion of models. For each model there are lots of different possible configurations such as monitor type, memory size and so on. The basics of computer hardware are described over the next few pages.

The computer

The older 8-bit machines such as the BBC 'B' are slower and have limited memory. They do, however, have lots of readily available software that has been proven in use, so it is still worth considering buying a BBC computer. Service and maintenance may, however, prove difficult. The newer machines, 16-bit or 32-bit, are faster, with much more memory, much of which is consumed by their enhanced features, such as better screen display. On the other hand, they are often better designed and therefore easier to learn how to use. They are also very expensive so purchases must be carefully planned. Two important issues to consider are suitability and compatibility. Will the machine be suitable for the purpose, i.e. is there lots of useful software? Will the machine be compatible with existing provision?

It is worth considering buying additional memory if this is an option. However, it is always possible to upgrade a system with additional memory. Memory is measured in kilobytes (kb) or megabytes (mb) : 1000 kb = 1mb. The amount of memory a computer has determines the speed and complexity of operation which it can undertake. Computer memory should not be confused with disk capacity which is also measured in kilobytes and megabytes. Disk capacity determines how much information can be stored on a disk, for example, I am currently using a 1 mb capacity disk which is just about adequate to contain all the text of this book.

Figure 3.2 reveals the proportions of the different leading makes of computer available to the modern languages teachers surveyed. Since the survey was mainly carried out in three LEAs the

32

figures are not representative of the national picture. What is of interest is the fact that the ratio of newer computers to older is 2:1.

The VDU

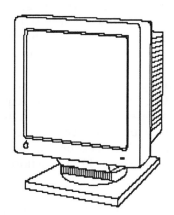

The Visual Display Unit (VDU), or screen, that you choose depends on the intended use. The types available vary not only in terms of size, black and white and colour, but also in resolution. Resolution refers to the number of dots on the screen, with the lowest resolution being the cheapest and giving the least clear image. A high resolution monitor can give a pin-sharp image. In making a purchasing decision, it is best to think in terms of what the monitor will be required to do. For word processing and mainly text-based activities a black and white monitor may give a clearer image than some low resolution colour monitors. However, in order to make use of software which uses colour graphics and / or exploits colour to structure and organise text-based programs, a high resolution colour monitor is required.

The disk drive

A disk drive is used in two ways:

• to read information from the disk and load into the computer
• to write information onto a disk.

This information might be in the form of a computer program, e.g. *Granville*, a text created by word processing, statistical data for use in a maths package, digitised sound or images, etc. A disk drive can be thought of as a cassette recorder which can play back or record information onto disks which can, in turn, be thought of as cassette tapes. As with cassettes, the information remains on the disk whether or not the machine is switched on but can be recorded over and irretrievably lost. Again, as with cassettes, disks have a security system to prevent the accidental erasure or overwriting of important data. This is known as write protection and its effect is to prevent any changes to the information on the disk. The existing information will be accessible, but no new information can be added to that disk. Of course, accidental damage is still possible, and it is recommended that for very valuable information there should be duplicate copies kept in different buildings.

There are three common types of disk drive, 5.25", 3.5" and hard drives. The first two accept floppy disks of the corresponding diameters. Paradoxically, the smaller 3.5" floppy disks are capable of holding more information than the larger 5.25" ones. Floppy disks can contain several thousand words of text which can be erased and rewritten many hundreds of times. Eventually, a floppy disk may become unreliable and possibly unuseable due to wear and tear, so back-up copies of important data are a necessity. Hard drives are increasingly common on school machines. They are much faster than floppy drives, can contain much more information, 20 to 100 times more, and are fixed in position. A common use of a hard drive is to store programs. For instance, my office machine contains the following software on the hard drive - a word processing package, a spreadsheet (which I use for accounts), a graphics package and modern languages software such as *Fun with texts* (Camsoft). The original copies of these programs were supplied on floppy disk and had to be installed (i.e. copied) onto the hard disk. This is a perfectly legal procedure, the instructions for which are usually contained in the program documentation. The hard drive can also be used to store files, such as text files created on a word processor. To avoid accidental loss, back-up copies of these should be kept on a floppy disk.

Given the variety of disk drives, various permutations are possible. The most basic is a single 5.25" drive as seen on many BBC computers. Some BBC drives are switchable between 40 and 80 tracks but many are not and can only work with disks formatted to 40 tracks. This leads to compatibility problems since an 80 track disk will not work on a 40 track drive and vice-versa. A drive which can be switched between 40 and 80 tracks is the solution. This problem is specific to BBC computers but typifies the lack of standardisation which bedevils computing. Another common disk drive configuration is a double 5.25" drive. This means that there are two floppy drives so it is possible to copy information from one drive to the other, rather like a twin-deck cassette recorder. It also means that more powerful applications can be run which draw information from disks in both drives without the laborious disk-swapping needed if only a single drive is available. Similar permutations are possible with 3.5" disk drives - a single drive or double drive. These drives are common on RM Nimbus, Apple Macintosh and Archimedes computers. As well as the capacity to contain more information than the larger disks, 3.5" disks also have the advantage of a more robust plastic casing.

Hard drives are most commonly found in schools fitted to network servers (the computer which runs the network) and on some computers in technology departments running computer aided design (CAD) software. For modern languages, it is certainly a useful feature, but unless major applications are to be run, such as high-powered word processing or desktop publishing packages, it is still not essential. The imminent arrival of high-quality sound may change that, but it is unclear whether the hard disk itself may be superseded by various new data storage formats, including compact disk (CD) drives. CD drives are now appearing in schools and it is predicted that by the end of 1992 all secondary schools will have at least one computer equipped with a CD drive. A CD drive can read programs and other data from CDs. Educational applications for CDs are beginning to appear with sound and pictures (including video) linked to computer programs.

The printer

Rapid advances in printer technology have brought high-quality output within reach. A printer must be regarded as an essential item since although programs can run without one, many of their advantages are lost. In fact, most modern languages teachers do regularly make use of a printer (see figure 3.3). A printer is useful, above all, if the pupils are producing text and/or graphics, because it enables them to have something to show for their efforts. The printers most commonly found in schools are of the dot matrix type. These are noisy in operation, give reasonable quality, do not present too many difficulties to operate and are relatively inexpensive to run. They use ribbons, akin to typewriter ribbons, which need frequent replacement to maintain print quality. Colour dot-matrix printers give reasonable results and do not cost that much more. Better known makes of printer such as Epson cost a little more, but the extra expense may be worth it since they are more likely to be fully compatible with the other hardware and the software that you will be using. Some cheaper printers are advertised as Epson compatible, this means that they will work with any software that is designed to work with an Epson printer.

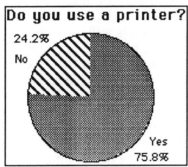

Figure 3.3

Laser printers offer the best quality of print and are quieter in operation than dot-matrix printers. They are, however, expensive to buy and maintain since toner cartridges need frequent replacement. Laser printers will only work with the more advanced computers and in view of their expense the prospective purchaser must ensure compatibility with hardware and software. It is probably best to buy computer, printer and software as part of a package. Ink-jet printers are quiet, reasonably cheap to buy and to operate and offer excellent quality. Their principle draw-back is in the area of compatibility with software. As yet, few schools have ink-jet printers and so software designers tend to overlook them. This may well change soon because of the obvious advantages of these printers. Colour ink-jet printers are also available. Daisy-wheel printers are found in some schools. These give good quality print-out for text but their inability to handle graphics greatly reduces their versatility. It is not necessary to buy a printer for every computer since they can be shared between two or more. In a network room, one printer usually serves all the computers. Some software packages are quite difficult to set up for use with some printers and expert advice may be required. This is a one-off operation and once it has been done it is no more difficult to use a printer than using any other reprographic equipment.

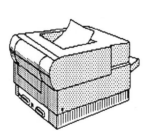

Laser printer

The mouse

A mouse is a device which makes using the computer a more intuitive process. As the mouse is moved across the surface of a desk, a pointer moves across the screen. For example, if a program offers the user a list or menu of options, the pointer may be moved to the desired option. In order to choose that option, the user then presses a button on the mouse. There are many ways in which the movement of the pointer and pressing of the button have been exploited by ingenious software designers. Word processing, graphics and desktop publishing are made much easier to understand and use with a mouse. The mouse is usually supplied with the computer but is well worth buying if offered as an optional extra. Of course, a mouse can easily be purchased later, but care should be taken to ensure that it is compatible with the software and hardware you already have. Some software does not exploit the mouse, but this is increasingly not the case. Apple Macintosh computers pioneered the mouse and these computers are seldom used without one. Mouse maintenance can be a problem - dirt and fluff clog their inner workings and young fingers soon learn how to remove the all important mouse ball - a hard rubber ball of great fascination to adolescents. The mouse is fitted as standard on many modern computers including RM Nimbus, Archimedes and Apple Mac. It is possible to use a mouse with older BBC machines but in practice there are very few BBC programs of interest in modern languages able to make use of a mouse.

The concept keyboard

As yet, only a minority of modern languages teachers have experience of using a concept keyboard. However, those that haven't feel that they have been missing out (see figures 3.4 and 3.5). A concept keyboard enables the user to give the computer instructions by pressing pads on a piece of hardware which looks like a board. The size of the pads is determined by the programmer. The surface of the concept keyboard is divided into small squares known as cells. One cell represents the smallest size of pad possible. The most common concept keyboards have 132 cells. Some more sophisticated keyboards can have up to 2000 cells. The concept keyboard is available in two sizes: A4 and A3. The choice of size depends on the use which is to be made of the keyboard. The use of the A3 keyboard suits younger pupils or

Figure 3.4

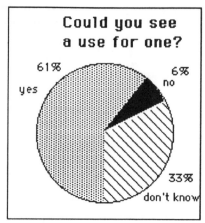

Figure 3.5

pupils with physical handicaps; older pupils might consider the A4 keyboard to be more mature. The overlay is a piece of paper, of the same size as the concept keyboard, on which there are visual clues as to what has been programmed for each cell. These clues can be words, phrases or pictures. For some activities, a blank overlay can be suitable.

Other hardware

The hardware components we have reviewed so far are the most commonly found items in schools. The computer, keyboard, VDU and disk drive are essential items without which nothing can be done. The printer, mouse and concept keyboard are all highly recommended additions to the basic system. There are many other items of hardware which are less commonly used in modern languages. Of these, the most important is probably the **modem**, although relatively few teachers seem to have used one or to envisage a use for one (see figures 3.6 and 3.7). This may be a result of unfamiliarity with the term 'modem'. In fact, it is a device which enables the computer to be connected via a telephone line to other computers. Electronic mail works in this way and has been used by some modern languages teachers to exchange letters with classes in other schools, whether at home or abroad. Electronic mail is specifically referred to in the MFL Order in AT3.5a which specifies the ability:

> *'to respond to texts ... eg. electronic mail messages from a penfriend,' (p.12).*

Another use of the modem is to connect to on-line databases such as *Campus 2000, Prestel* and the French *Minitel.* There is a great deal of potential in this field in terms of both teaching and learning materials. Although modems are relatively inexpensive, their potential remains largely unrealised because of the other expenses involved. Schools are not in a position to run up the large 'phone bills that extensive use of the modem would lead to, especially if modern languages departments are frequently using *Minitel* and its equivalents in other European countries. There is also the additional cost of subscriptions if

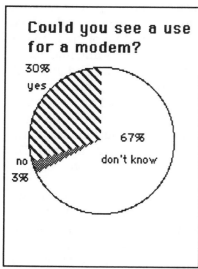

Figure 3.6

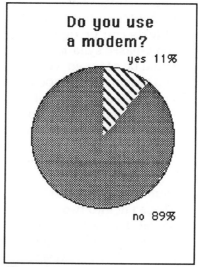

Figure 3.7

one wishes to use the services of *Campus 2000* or other services such as *NERIS* - which stores up-to-date and easily searched lists of teaching and learning materials. This facility could soon put an end to the days of wading through catalogues! The question of funding for such resources was addressed by the Final Report which called for special assistance to meet:

> *'...the running costs of electronic mail.'* *(Para. 17.24.)*

An alternative to electronic mail which runs on similar principles is Fax.

There are a variety of ways of producing speech on school micros. **Speech synthesizers** can be bought fairly cheaply for use with the BBC. French and German versions are available and these are worth considering. The quality is dalek-like but better than nothing and has been used, particularly with visually-handicapped children, as a way of providing access to IT. The synthesizers work by converting text to its phonetic sound. Another way of using sound is to digitally record the sound so that it can then be saved in the computer's memory or on disk. This facility is built into the latest Apple Macintosh computers and is available as an add-on for others, such as the PCs (including RM Nimbus and Archimedes computers). The computer is able to function as a cassette recorder but with the facility to play back instantly any piece of the recording. Classroom uses of this facility are beginning to emerge.

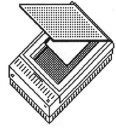

A scanner

The **scanner** is a device which allows images to be digitised so that they are then available for use with various software applications (a case in point is case study 1.11). The facility could be of great use in the preparation of teaching and learning materials. A refinement of the use of a scanner is the addition of Optical Character Recognition software, for example *Omnipage* (Formscan UK). This allows texts to be scanned, digitised and then converted back to text. In other words, it allows texts to be placed onto the computer without the need for retyping. In this way, a database of texts can be rapidly acquired which could be of great use in topic-based syllabuses. Articles from newspapers and magazines could be scanned, copyright problems permitting, and an excellent resource developed. In one local authority, a project is under way to create a central resource bank of scanned articles which is accessible by all secondary schools in the authority via cable links. The bank of articles can be searched in various ways, the user can read the article on screen and, if desired, print it out. The use of a laser printer gives a similar quality to a photo-copy.

Cameras which can be used with computers are also available. These fall into two categories - analogue and digital. The *Dycam Model 1* is an example of a digital still camera. It has the appearance of an ordinary compact camera with autofocus and built-in flash. However, when connected to an Apple Macintosh or IBM compatible (including RM Nimbus and Archimedes) computer the photographs can be displayed on screen. They can then be used in desktop publishing packages to provide illustrations.

The *Canon Ion* still video camera is an analogue camera. It has the advantage of full colour and the facility to work not only with a computer but also with an ordinary television set. The potential for creating visual aids is enormous. An adapter is also available for the *Canon Ion* which allows 35mm negatives to be converted so that all your old photographs of French road signs can be displayed on a television screen or incorporated into computer packages. The *Canon Ion* will also store images onto video tape. Sound can then be added to create the equivalent of tape / slide shows.

For children with special educational needs, devices are available which make it possible for them to use a computer. These include speech synthesizers, voice sensitive devices, specially adapted input devices, etc. Without such hardware some children would be denied access to the National Curriculum. This is clearly acknowledged in the MFL Order (p. 1):

> *'Pupils unable to communicate by speech may use other means including the use of technology, signing, symbols or lip-reading as alternatives to speaking and listening. ... The use of technological aids by pupils who depend on them physically to produce their written work is acceptable.'*

Hardware policy   What is a suitable level of resourcing for a modern languages department? Before we consider this, it must be acknowledged that most departments are in a far from ideal situation in terms of IT resourcing and that there is no immediate prospect for change. Where a school policy on access to IT has been established, it is possible for a modern languages faculty to plan its use of the resource much more sensibly. LEA guidelines on the formulation of school policy can help ensure that the modern languages faculty does not lose out to other curricular areas. There is much excellent practice in which the limited resources available are exploited in imaginative ways. One very basic and ancient computer can be used to very good effect as many of the case studies show. By demonstrating the value of IT in this way, we are making an excellent case for further resourcing and taking modern languages from Cinderella status, as far as use of IT is concerned, to a point where a case for some degree of priority is clearly established, so that departments are then able to demand such facilities as they might require. In each department, one would want a number of trolley-based machines, perhaps one or two per teaching room or per member of staff. Such provision would allow the occasional pooling of the resources to allow a number of machines to be used in one room. Each of these machines should be equipped with a concept keyboard. For each room, a printer would be required and within the department there should be access to a double disk drive. Some modern

languages faculties have established small resource rooms equipped with computers, listening stations and the like. Students come out of class to use these facilities. Access to whole school facilities such as a network room, modem, laser printer, scanner and CD drive completes this ideal picture.

Software

In addition to the hardware described above, software, or computer programs, must also be purchased. Here the choices are far wider and the distinctions between different types much more nebulous. From a modern languages perspective, software can be divided into two broad areas comprising, on the one hand, subject specific software designed exclusively or primarily for use in language learning, and on the other hand, applications designed for general use.

Subject specific software

This category includes vocabulary, grammar and comprehension testing programs, simulations such as *Granville* (Camsoft), games, foreign language adventures and others such as *Quelle tête* (Camsoft). As indicated in Chapter 1, this type of software is less likely to meet the requirements of the National Curriculum, although in some cases it will, where the software amounts to an emulation of a standard application as with some of the dedicated databases. Some of the better known programs are listed below.

French	BBC	Nimbus	Arc	Mac
Granville	√	√	√	
Quelle tête	√			
Jeu des ménages	√			
Databanks (A l'hôtel, Au camping, etc)	√	√	In the pipeline?	
A vous la France	√			
Six French games	√			
Connections	√			
German				
Kopfjäger	√			
Umziehen	√			
Databanks (Im Hotel, Im Restaurant)	√	√	In the pipeline?	
Deutsch Direkt	√			
German Games	√			
French German Spanish English				
Hotel Excelsior	√	√	√	

Figure 3.8

Applications   General applications of particular interest in modern languages include text manipulation programs, word processing, desktop publishing, databases, spreadsheets, graphics programs and concept keyboard applications. Perhaps the best known text manipulation program is *Fun with texts* (Camsoft) but there are numerous others as figure 3.9 shows. Text manipulation programs enable the user to perform relatively simple operations such as gap-filling, anagrams, line rearranging, matching, etc - in fact, many of the exercises familiar in language learning using the basic technology of pencil and paper. The computer brings various advantages. Firstly, the task is managed by the computer in terms of explanation, presentation, marking and storage. Secondly, a large number of texts can be worked upon. These may be developed locally or bought in - increasingly, publishers are producing texts which operate with programs like *Fun with texts* (Camsoft), as an integral part of their course. Furthermore, the student who uses such software can have as many goes as he or she likes, but the text is always neatly presented in a standard format so that it can't be 'mucked up'. For AT3.5b the example given in the Final Report was:

> *'Predict the correct sequence of words in a text*
> *using text manipulation software.' (P.29.)*

This example has been omitted in the MFL Order, but the use of computers would be appropriate for this statement of attainment. Other authoring packages enable the user to devise wordsearches, crosswords, tests, etc.

	LANGUAGES	BBC	Nimbus	Arc	Mac
Fun with texts	F G S I R E	√	√	√	In the pipeline
Match Master	F G S	√	√		√
Gapmaster	F G S	√	√		√
Question master	F G S E		√	√	√
Tray	E	√	√ (2 versns)		
Muddles	E		√		
Newsroom Extra	E	√	√		
Crossword Call-up	E	√		√	
Wordsearcher	E	√			
Cartoon		√			
Storyboard	E F G S I	√			
Word Sequencing	F G	√	√	√	√

Figure 3.9

There are many different word processing programs available and the choice will depend upon the intended use. Many schools will endeavour to standardise across the curriculum on a particular word processing package. It is to everyone's advantage if the pupils are able to practise and consolidate their word processing skills in the different subjects. Languages teachers will wish to ensure that the program chosen allows accented characters to be used. In addition to the school's standard program, modern languages teachers may want to use other specialist word processing software such as foreign language versions (screen messages and instructions displayed in the foreign language). For AT4.8c the example in the MFL Order concludes:

> '...write up the results of the survey using a wordprocessor.' (P.16.)

Programs include:

	Languages	BBC	Nimbus	Arc	Mac
Folio	F G	√			
Asian Folio	Pa Guj H B	√			
Allwrite	F G I S R Pa Guj Hi Be Gr Tu Tamil A Farsi U		√		
Minnie	F G Sp		√		
Prompt/Writer	E	√	√		
Stylus	E	√			
Macwrite	F G S E				√
View	E	√			
Flexiwrite	E			√	
First word plus	F G S E I			√	
Arabic Macintosh	A				√
Rustext	R	√		√	
Red Square	R		√	√	

Figure 3.10

Desktop publishing

Desktop publishing involves the use of text and/or graphics to prepare and print posters, handbills, articles, newspapers, brochures, indeed anything that might be printed out. The production of teaching and learning materials is an obvious use for desktop publishing. Pupils might use desktop publishing to produce brochures and many other items. For AT1.7b the MFL Order gives the following example:

> 'Listen to the news headlines and produce the outline of a newspaper's front page using desktop publishing software.' (P.4.)

Again, it is important that pupils acquire transferable skills since it would not be a cost effective use of modern languages curriculum time to learn how to use a desktop publishing program. The following desktop publishing packages are commonly used in schools:

	Languages	BBC	Nimbus	Arc	Mac
Front Page Europe	F G I S	√			
NewSpaper	E		√		
Caxton Press	E		√		
Aldus Pagemaker	F G S E		√	√	√

Figure 3.11

Graphics

These programs enable the user to draw pictures on the VDU which may then be printed out. This kind of software works well only with 16 bit and 32 bit computers and a mouse is essential. Some modern languages teachers use this facility as a reading or listening comprehension exercise. As well as drawing an original picture, the user can edit or add to an existing one. Some packages enable objects to be moved around the screen, a facility which can be used to support role-play. Programs of note include:

Paintspa (SPA)
MacDraw (Claris)
Collage (MUSE)
Artisan (Clares).

Databases

A host of modern languages learning activities can be devised for use with databases, as the case studies show. Pupils can be given tasks which involve searching databases for information, collecting information to enter into an existing database or creating a new database. A database is essentially an electronic filing system. Its power derives from the computer's ability to rapidly check through files searching for information. For AT3.8a the example given in the MFL Order includes:

> *'...obtain information about less familiar subjects by selecting and consulting computer databases.' (P.12).*

AT1.7a also contains a reference to databases:

> *'...add to a database on a foreign town based on information from a foreign visitor,' (p.4).*

	Languages	BBC	Nimbus	Arc	Mac
ML Find	F G I S W	√	√		
French Grass	F	√	√		
German Grass	G	√	√		
Grass	E (fields in any)	√	√	√	
Hypercard	All				√
Genesis	E F G S			√	

Figure 3.12

Concept keyboard software

Concept match (NCET, NW SEMERC) enables the pupils to match the message which appears on the monitor screen with a visual clue on the overlay. The visual clue can be a picture, a word or a phrase. The MFL Order envisages the use of such software in AT3.1a:

> *'Match labels and pictures using a keyboard overlay.' (P.11.)*

Prompt/Writer (NCET) are two simple word processors which allow pupils to write through the ordinary keyboard or the concept keyboard.

Stylus is another simple word processor which can be used with the ordinary keyboard and/or the concept keyboard.

Touch Explorer Plus (NCET) is a sophisticated piece of software which gives access to six different levels. These can be used to differentiate work in terms of difficulty; they can also provide different types of information and thus turn the program into a simple database. If used with a BBC Master, *Touch Explorer Plus* has a built-in word processor which makes it possible to manipulate the information. Another facility makes it possible to hear the messages on the screen through a Speech Synthesizer.

List Explorer (NCET) is a simple database which is manipulated find it difficult to operate through words only as the clues provided on the overlay can be pictorial. This database allows the retrieval of data as well as the creation of a new database.

To use the above programs in modern languages special files and overlays are required. These can be home-produced but some are now being published. For example:

Eautun (Hereford and Worcester IT Service)
The Environment (FLIP Project, Liverpool)
Materials from Nelson & Co.

Miscellaneous

A wide range of other types of software can be used in modern languages. These include:

Teletype emulators can be an effective tool for managing a classroom activity. Messages are displayed on screen and, if a printer is connected, printed out at variable time intervals. Programs:

Teletype (Sherston)
Simtex (ILECC)
Extra! (SECC)

Viewdata emulators make it possible to create information screens linked by numbered pages on the model of the teletext services we see on TV, i.e. *CEEFAX* and *Oracle*. Viewdata displays are also common in many other areas such as traffic information, tourist information and advertising. A case study is included in chapter three of how a group of children used a service for their exchange school who were visiting them. Programs:

Simtex (ILECC)
News Bulletin (Newman)

Spreadsheets are used to record statistical information and perform rapid and complex calculations. For AT3.7b the MFL Order gives the following example:

> *'Read to extract (or select) details from programmes, timetables, posters and spreadsheets...' (p.12).*

Spreadsheets are particularly useful in keeping accounts and this means they can be used in modern languages to create work-related tasks. Another use is to provide a means of rapidly converting prices from one currency to another and up-dating these as the exchange rates change.

Electronic-mail emulators make it is possible to connect two computers by cable to emulate electronic mail. Program:

Chatter. (NCET, NW SEMERC)

What if I don't teach French?

The range of teaching and learning materials available for French is much wider than for other languages taught in Britain. It could hardly be expected to be much different in IT. Where packages have been specifically developed for language learning they are generally in French. Sometimes there is a German version and occasionally a Spanish one. It is rare to find anything in a language other than the three most commonly taught ones.

However, the picture is not quite as bleak as it sounds. Some software can be readily adapted to run in several languages. Word processing is a case in point. Words can be typed in any language. Foreign accents are not always available, although many programs do have them. There are even some packages which support alphabets other than the Roman, for instance *Allwrite* (ILECC) and *Folio* (EDS). These support such languages as Urdu, Panjabi, Greek and Russian.

Another route open to the teacher of the lesser taught languages is to obtain software designed to be run in the countries where that language is spoken. An example of this would be *Arabic Macintosh* (Diwan).

Another possibility is to use software which is not text based. Graphics packages can be used as listening or reading comprehension exercises. The students follow the instructions to create a picture on screen. Spreadsheets can be used similarly except that the students are now manipulating columns of figures.

Finally, English packages can be used in information gap activities. For example, an English database giving local tourist information is used to find the information requested by a foreign visitor. The student operating the database might be asked in Panjabi for the names of hotels with rooms vacant. He or she searches the database, finds the information and then has to respond to the tourist in the target language - in this case Panjabi.

Software summary

Teachers who took part in the survey carried out for this chapter were convinced of the usefulness of word processing and text manipulation above other applications. Databases, games, electronic mail and desktop publishing were all considered useful by most respondents. The greatest uncertainty concerned graphics packages and adventures. Figure 3.13 summarises how teachers felt about the usefulness of the applications listed.

Software Top 9

1 **word processing**
2 **text manipulation**
3 **databases**
4 **games**
5 **desktop publishing**
6 **simulations**
7 **electronic mail**
8 **adventures**
9 **graphics**

Figure 3.13

For more information about software consult one of the following:

NERIS - this service is available in a number of schools either via *Campus 2000* or on a CD. *NERIS* is a database of teaching and learning materials which can quickly be searched and gives comprehensive details about all items stored on it as the following print-out shows. *NERIS* stores details about a wide range of subjects and covers materials in all media.

AVP - a commercial publisher which also acts as a distributor for a wide range of independent software producers. AVP make much of their software available on approval so you can try before you buy. For a catalogue contact AVP, School Hill Centre, Chepstow, Gwent, NP6 5PH. (tel: 0291 625439)

CILT - the CILT library stocks many IT applications and these can be tried out there.

NCET produce regular modern languages information sheets giving details of software and many other aspects of using IT in modern languages. These information sheets are available from the information officer at NCET who also operates an information service which can help you find out about software and hardware availability.

See also the list of addresses in appendix 3.

Chapter 4
Case studies

The case studies in this chapter have been compiled from many different sources. They are offered here as examples of the interesting ways in which some teachers are using IT. These ideas can be taken and adapted in many ways. If the software mentioned in a particular case study is not available for a given make of computer, there will usually be an equivalent package. Even if certain ideas are not easily replicable because of local constraints, they should at least provide food for thought. The key to developing IT activities is an appreciation of what can be done using the various applications wedded to a strong sense of what makes good sense in terms of language learning. In addition to the case studies there are some suggested ideas for activities. Some of the case studies can be seen in action on a video *IT in the languages classroom* (NCET).

Note: Each case study is marked by one or more symbols to indicate the appropriate Attainment Target(s). These are based on the four skills:

AT1: listening: the development of pupils' ability to understand and respond to spoken language.

AT2: speaking: the development of pupils' ability to communicate in speech.

AT3: reading: the development of pupils' ability to read and respond to written language.

AT4: writing: the development of pupils' ability to communicate in writing.

1 Word processing

1.1 Story writing

A Year 11 top set class in a comprehensive school. This school was following the Southern Examining Group's Modular French GCSE syllabus. One of the modules includes work on accidents and *gîtes*. Some imaginative stories were produced using Minnie. The class first did some listening work relating to the proprietor welcoming his guests to a *gîte*. For the next lesson, the school's 16 station Nimbus network room was booked. The pupils, working in pairs, were presented with a screen which contained the opening paragraph for the story. This had been typed in by the teacher who had also prepared words and phrases to help the pupils (see figure 4.1). These could be displayed on screen and entered into the text by operating the mouse.

RED

je	mon père a
j'ai	mon père est
je suis	ma mère a
nous avons	ma mère est
nous sommes	il y a

ma soeur a	le propriétaire
ma soeur est	le propriétaire a
j'ai dû	il faut
nous avons dû	
le propriétaire est	

GREEN

ouvert	perdu	laissé tomber
fermé	renversé	débranché
déchiré	dit	
brûlé	allé	
cassé	téléphoné	

avait	fumais	réparer
c'était	buvais	nettoyer
était	regardais	faire
mettais	laver	passer
faisais	remplacer	

YELLOW

un placard	une assiette
une nappe	un drap
une bouteille	une couverture
un verre	un tapis
un couteau	le frigidaire

la machine à laver	le lit
la prise de courant	le vélo
la cuisinière	l'évier
l'aspirateur	le robinet
la moquette	le rideau

une auréole
une tâche
de la boue
du sang
un trou

BLUE

furieux	hélas	soudain
fâché	après ça	tout d'un coup
sympa	ensuite	tout de suite
puis	enfin	finalement
quand	pendant que	

quel désastre	un peu plus tard
quelle horreur	
la catastrophe	
malheureusement	
cinq minutes plus tard	

In *Minnie* there are four colour-coded boxes (red, green, yellow and blue) each of which can hold a number of pages (page division represented by a dotted line)

Figure 4.1

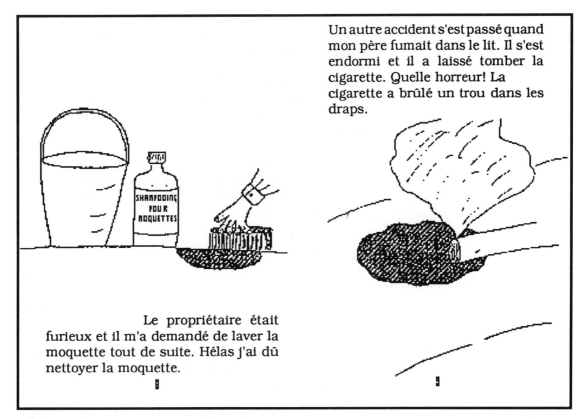

Figure 4.2

The task was to complete the story. As well as the words supplied via the *Minnie* (MUSE) word boxes, the pupils also used dictionaries and consulted the teacher and student teacher, who was on an observation visit.

The following is an example of one of the more way-out stories produced:

> *Me voilà dans un gîte en France. Le gîte est excellent ou plutôt le gîte était excellent! Malheureusement nous avons eu quelques petits accidents. Nous regardions un match de football a la télé quand Chris Waddle a marqué un but pour Marseille. Nous avons sauté et nous avons crié. Puis, 'BANG' ma main a frappé une vase. La vase est tombé et elle a cassé sur la moquette et maintenant, il y a une aureole.*
>
> *Pendant ce temps, mon frère était dans la cuisinière. Il a obtenu un bronzage. Malheureusement, ma mère a preparé nos dîners et elle a mis un poulet dans la cuisinière. Mon frère a crié "NON, NON JE SUIS ICI!!!!" Puis ma mère a laissé tomber le poulet, et elle a brulé la reine d'Angleterrre qui était ici pour nous rendre visite.*

Hier j,étais en votre vélo quand j'ai eu un petit accident. Je descendais la rue quand un hamster a décidé de traverser la rue. Il est allé devant moi. J'ai écrasé l'hamster alors, il a mangé mon pneu. Avant ça je l'ai demandé l'hamster pour de l'argent mais il a dit "TANT PIS, JE SUIS MORT!!!"

Ah non!, ma mère a brulé le gîte. Ne vous en faites pas, ce n'est pas grave, c'est juste un petit trou! Je vais réparer ça avec un morceau de papier hygiénique.

Oops, maintenant il pleut et tuot le monde est mouillé!!

Au revoir.

(Pupils' uncorrected first draft)

In the next lesson, the pupils improvised role-plays in which one of them took the part of the enraged *gîte* owner and the other one of the accident-prone guests.

Subsequently, with the help of NCET, the teacher of this class decided to set about making the stories this class produced into small illustrated booklets (see figure 4.2). The booklets are now in the school library and are very popular. (These booklets have now been published for NCET by RLDU, Sheridan Road, Bristol.)

The teacher concerned has varied this idea by asking children from a different class to do the illustrations so that they read the stories with a clear purpose and respond to them through their drawing. There has also been collaboration with the art department with regard to techniques for illustration.

1.2 Play scripts

A year 9 class listened to a sound recording of a simple sketch made by the teacher with the help of the foreign language assistant. The script of this play had been made into a gap filling exercise using a word processing package. After this, pupils were given a more skeletal form of the same text and encouraged to improvise the detail in order to come up with original scripts which could then be enacted. As this class grew used to working in this way, they were able to tackle a more ambitious co-operative play writing exercise in which teams of writers worked on different aspects of the script. The cut and paste facilities offered by the word processing package were adequate to stitch all the parts into a cohesive whole before printing out and copying the final script. The pupils then learned their parts prior to acting them out.

1.3 Chain stories

Using a word processing package the teacher wrote the opening paragraph of a story. The students then continued the story sentence by sentence. However, after each sentence they moved onto the next computer. In this way composite stories were built up. When necessary, prompts were given for each new sentence such as who was the main character? what was he/she like? where did he/she live? etc. As a concluding activity some purposeful reading occurred as the pupils revisited each computer in turn to review the final outcome. The print-out was made into an instant anthology.

If only one or two computers are available the activity can be modified to produce just one or two stories. The class works in groups and each group takes a turn at the computer(s) as a part of a carousel including other non-computer activities.

1.4 Writing a poem

A common technique for teaching children to write a poem is to provide a simple model structure and a pool of words to build into it. A year 8 class produced poems in this way using *Minnie*. The model for the poems was:

adjective snow falling adverb

The colour coded boxes of *Minnie* were used to offer lists of adjectives in one coloured box and adverbs in a box of a different colour. The finished results were printed out and illustrated. Many variations are possible simply by changing the middle two words, e.g. fish swimming, lambs playing, sun shining, rain falling, children crying, soldiers fighting, etc.

1.5 Pen pal letters I

Two low ability year 10 classes worked on producing advertisements for a pen pal. They used *Minnie* to do this and printed out the advertisements in one of the large fonts available which made an effective classroom wall display when all of the advertisements were pasted up. Only the teachers knew the identities of the advertisers which they recorded by giving a number to each advertisement. In the following lesson the pupils selected an advertisement to reply to and begin their reply *Cher numéro 1* etc. The most popular advertisers received the most replies. Two examples of these replies are given below. By virtue of the fact that they were using a somewhat extended version of the original *Minnie* file for the letters, the pupils were on familiar ground with the software support it offered.

> Cher numéro 6
>
> Je m'appelle Oliver.
> J'habite à Kingswood, près de Bristol.
> J'ai quatorze ans. J'ai une soeur. Je joue au golf tous les weekends. Je regarde le football tous les weekends. Je regarde la télévision tous les jours. J'écoute la musique pop tous les jours. Je déteste la natation et

Cher numéro 11
Je m'appelle SIMON FORD j'habite à
Pucklechurch près de Bristol. J'ai
quatorze ans. J'ai un frère Nick, Nick
a treize ans. Je vais à la pêche avec
mes amis. J'écoute la musique heavy
metal. Je regarde la télévision avec
mes amis tous les weekends. je déteste
le golf, le snooker et la natation.

1.6 Pen pals II

A year 11 class used cue cards for a role play in which they discussed a recent holiday in France. They then wrote a letter to a pen pal in France describing that holiday. To do this they used *Minnie.* The word boxes provided support and structure. The students used the vocabulary of the word boxes in unexpected ways, for instance, items of food and drink had been included for them to write about meals but were adapted for use in writing about souvenirs they had brought back.

1.7 Pen pals III

A year 9 Italian class watched a video made by their link school in La Spezia in which the various members of the class introduced themselves and described their likes, dislikes, hobbies, etc. The pupils had to decide which of the people they would like to write to. These video letters were typed onto the computer by the teacher using a word processing package. The pupils then read the letter that they wished to answer from the VDU and with the help of a prompt card supplied by the teacher made notes to help organise their reply which they wrote using the word processor. The final printed versions of the letters were mailed to the Italian youngsters. This case study is on the NCET video (part 2 extract 2).

1.8 Newspapers

A class newspaper is an obvious way of publishing the writing of students. There are numerous examples of newsroom simulations in which the students produce their newspaper in real time. In one recent case the students received incoming messages by electronic mail. The stories had to be rewritten, edited and given headlines. They were then cut and pasted using a desk top publishing package to produce a high quality final product. This is a fairly major enterprise and required the co-ordination of a local education authority's specialist advisory services.

Another way of workingis to produce a class magazine over a period of time, perhaps one academic year. Students use a word processing package to produce articles in each of the different topic areas in which they work - sport, weather, crime, accidents, traffic, politics, disasters, entertainment, etc. A desk top publishing program or scissors and paste can be used to make the final product.

1.9 Business letters

The following exercise has been used with a variety of pupils in the 14-18 age group working at a wide range of levels. A group of three pupils work with two computers in a simulation of an export manager's office. One of the computers is running a telex simulation. From time to time messages appear in English on the VDU of this computer from the export manager who is travelling abroad on business. The first message requests that a letter be sent in French to a company in Belgium arranging a visit there by the export manager. Rather than type the whole letter the students have to edit the file copy for his last visit to the Belgian company which they call up on the second computer and edit using a word processing package. Subsequently, another message appears which announces a change of plan. Due to an unforeseen circumstance the export manager will not be able to make the visit but his assistant will substitute for him on a different day. The letter must be redrafted for a second time. In fact, the new set of arrangements correspond closely to those in the original file copy so that those who have worked more slowly have less to redraft. This provides an element of differentiation which would enable slower workers to complete as much of the task as faster ones.

This activity is one of a number of work related tasks contained in the pack of materials called *The 1992 Experience* (St. Martin's College).

1.10 Captions I

A year 11 class in a special school used a concept keyboard overlay and the program *Concept Match* (NCET) to practise matching the weather vocabulary they had learned orally with its written form. The weather phrases appeared on screen and they had to press the correct picture on the overlay. Using the same overlay but with the program *Prompt/Writer* (NCET) they were able to 'write' these phrases simply by pressing on the overlay. The phrases were printed out and cut up to be used as captions for the students' weather pictures(see page 54).

This very simple task proved a rewarding early step for these students in their second year of learning French. The school staff found that, contrary to their expectations, through the use of IT, writing could be an integral part of their scheme of work and that, more importantly, the pupils' learning was reinforced both in terms of French and basic literacy. These students went on to use more complicated overlays which enabled them to build up short texts. (See NCET video part 2 extract 4).

1.11 Captions 2

The program *Caption* (NCET) allows pupils to insert text onto a picture which is displayed on screen. A number of screen pictures are supplied with the software but others can be produced.

One enterprising advisory teacher has worked with the local IT centre to produce electronically scanned images from sources such as Tin Tin books. If the captioned picture is printed out on a colour printer the final results are extremely impressive.

1.12 Menus

Two student teachers created a file for *Minnie* which enabled them to produce Spanish menus with a range of classes. The file gives access to lists of courses, dishes and drinks. The words in these lists can be moved into a menu format by manipulating the mouse with no need to retype them. Using the software, the menus were embellished with borders and then printed out in a large range of fonts (print styles). The final product was used in role play, for display and as a record of pupils' work. This was basically a sorting and matching exercise but with pupils free to select which dishes they would have in their restaurant. They could also type in other dishes if they wished.

The following two case studies are taken from a forthcoming NCET publication, 'Look - my language is on the computer.'

1.13. Using Panjabi Folio

Although New Commonwealth immigrants began to settle in Southall before 1960, in Villiers High School Asian pupils became more conspicuous only after comprehensive re-organisation took place in 1974. Before this re-organisation Villiers High School was a Grammar School for selected pupils and few Asian pupils were admitted. A large majority of pupils in the present intake are from Asian families and approximately 80% of pupils are of Sikh origin coming mainly from the Punjab in Northern India. A considerable number came from East Africa and Singapore or Malaysia. Panjabi is the main non-English language spoken in Southall. The vast majority of pupils are bilingual or multilingual. The school recognises the cultural diversity of its pupils and encourages them to develop a greater awareness of the culture of their parents as well as that of the host community. Due to its linguistic make-up the school has made provision for languages in years 8 and 9. Pupils opt for one language from a set of modern European languages, for example French, German, Spanish and one from community languages, for example Panjabi, Hindi, Urdu. In years 10 and 11 pupils select which of the two languages they wish to study for a GCSE certificate. Last year more than sixty pupils took Panjabi at GCSE. Nearly the same number is opting for it this year. There is also provision for 'A' level Panjabi at the school. To maintain and promote interest in community languages, the school has provided wordprocessing facilities in Panjabi through the use of the Panjabi fonts in *Folio*. Pupils are encouraged to use the wordprocessor and most of the materials and children's work are wordprocessed. In January 1991, *Asian Folio* (ESM) was introduced into the mainstream computer studies course so that not only are the facilities available to pupils but the expertise is also there to support their efforts.

1.14. Bilingual story books

This idea for bilingual story books developed during a summer term several years ago. It started as a way of exploring a theme of communications for year 7 children in their final term. It was also an attractive, lasting idea which the children could work on and leave behind them as a resource when they left. The gradual introduction of the bilingual aspect of the books came as a direct result of community language support from within the school. The children had been confidently using *Folio* for some time and it seemed a natural development to use this skill, with guidance, to include translations of their own books. It also gave us a chance to bring Panjabi into the mainstream classroom for all children to experience in a very practical and positive way. The books themselves were always aimed at a younger audience and the ideas had to be as original as possible. The children worked in small groups of three or four so that the quite onerous task of producing the pictures was shared. The story was prepared in rough and redrafted as necessary. The translation would then take place, usually into Panjabi but on occasions into Urdu or Hindi. When this stage was reached the demand for computers became quite high as the printing stage could not be rushed for fear of ruining a picture. Where possible a second computer was used so that text in English could be completed on one while text in Panjabi was being completed on another. The complete story was always typed in and saved and then the page length altered so that each individual page could be printed separately. Despite great care being taken mistakes did occur and this would sometimes mean an entire picture being redrawn. The children took great pride in this work and because they were able to leave their names as authors and illustrators on the books, it gave them quite a sense of achievement.

Suggested activity

1.15 Multiple choice story

As a preliminary step to writing stories of their own, students could work on a form of cloze exercise to produce individualised stories. The gaps in the cloze exercise should be primarily nouns - the characters and where they live. For each space in the text a number of possible answers are required. The student has free choice but is constrained by the need to create a sensible story.

Cloze packages could be used but a word processor is preferable because it gives greater scope for students to add to the story, printing and other options are easier, there is no need for one correct answer and the IT element could be considered more authentic.

A story might begin as follows:

> *Once upon a time there was a prince / wizard /*
> *monster. He lived in a cave / palace / cottage.*
> *One day he went to the forest / lake / dungeons.*

If *Minnie* was to be used for this, the suggested words could be given in the boxes.) The students use the delete key to erase unwanted options. They also type in their own ideas. Students should not need much encouraging to finish off their story with their own ending. As a next step, characters of different genders might be included to create a grammatical puzzle.

2 Text manipulation programs

2.1 Flexible learning I

A year 7 mixed ability class in an inner city school. The class worked on the topic of post-cards with four different but complementary activities, only one of which was IT-based. The activities were: talk cards; writing a post-card; a reading comprehension based on an authentic brochure; using *Fun with texts* (Camsoft) on the computer. The activities were tackled by the pupils in the order they chose, but the teacher controlled the sequence in which they worked at the computer in threes. The teacher felt that another computer would have helped. The lesson was purposeful and varied with a high degree of learner autonomy and little pressure for control. The IT activity was based on a post card-style letter written by the teacher. The pupils were able to read the text through before it was hidden, using the 'Copywrite' option provided by *Fun With Texts*. This replaces all letters apart from capitals by a dash. The pupils can guess any of the words and if they guess correctly the word is inserted at every occurrence. This option is slightly harder than the prediction option which the teacher encouraged the less able pupils to use. In this, the text is hidden completely. The pupils then have to guess each word in sequence from a choice of five offered to them. This IT activity was well integrated into the overall scheme of things and helped the teacher by providing an autonomous, self-correcting activity. (See NCET video part 2 extract 1).

2.2 Flexible learning II

Three parallel groups of year 10 students of GCSE German, each group comprising 20 to 23 students, worked in the school's Nimbus network room over the course of two 50-minute lessons. They were working on the topic of holidays and used *Fun With Texts* and *Word Sequencing*. The IT work served as reinforcement to previously introduced material (from the overhead projector) and oral pair work, which included question / answer structures on: location of holiday; reason(s) for choice; accommodation; timing; people with whom individual is travelling. Half the group began with the *Word Sequencing* (Camsoft) file from English cues as follows:

1 Wohin fährst du?
2 Was machst du in den Sommerferien?
3 Wie lange bleibst du dort?
4 Was für Unterkunft habt ihr?
5 Mit wem fährst du nach Italien?
6 Ich bleibe drei Wochen in der Türkei.
7 Ich fahre mit meinen Eltern in Urlaub.

57

8 Wir fahren mit dem Wagen nach Rom.
9 Ich schwimme im Meer und lese Romane.
10 Wir fahren mit der Fähre nach Calais.
11 Mein Bruder fährt Anfang Juli mit seiner
Freundin in Urlaub.
12 Ich lege mich gern in die Sonne auf dem
Strand.

How would you ask/state the following?

1 Ask where someone is going.
2 Ask what someone is doing in the summer
holidays.
3 Ask how long someone is staying there.
4 Ask what sort of accommodation a group
has.
5 Ask someone who s/he is travelling to Italy
with.
6 Say you are staying in Turkey for three
weeks.
7 Say you are going on holiday with your
parents.
8 Say you (a group) are going to Rome by car.
9 Say you swim in the sea and read novels.
10 Say you (a group) are going to Calais by
ferry.
11 Say your brother is going on holiday with his
girlfriend at the beginning of July.
12 Say you like sunbathing on the beach.

The other half first listened to a taped dialogue on personal stereos making notes on the dialogue on a worksheet. Running these two activities concurrently was determined by nothing more profound than the limited number of personal stereos available! After completing the listening exercise and making sufficient notes the students moved on to the *Fun With Texts* file below:

Monika Hüttner fährt jedes Jahr in Urlaub. Sie
fährt meistens in die Schweiz, weil sie die Alpen
gern hat und auch weil sie nur deutsch sprechen
kann. Nächsten Sommer möchte sie aber nach
Österreich fahren. Da hat sie eine ältere Tante
und sie kann bei ihr übernachten. Sie fährt mit
dem Zug nach Salzburg, wo die Tante Liesl
wohnt, weil sie Auto fahren haßt. Sie fährt Mitte
Juni, bevor es zu viele Touristen gibt, und bleibt
ungefähr vierzehn Tage dort. Monika findet den
Akzent und das Essen in Österreich sehr
interessant.

The students used the 'Textsalad' (line reordering) exercise initially, so that they could quickly see the whole text in full. They then manipulated the text a second time in a more complex form (e.g. 'Prediction' or 'Copywrite'). Those who began with the listening exercise moved on to the *Word Sequencing* file and vice versa.

2.3 Text manipulation lesson

A lower set year 10 French class spent a whole double period, 70 minutes, working hard at the sequence of tasks given below. The teacher used *Fun with Texts* running on BBC micros which were not networked. The teacher had written a simple text which was a self-description of a fictional pupil of similar age and background to that of the class. The pupils worked in pairs on this text throughout but used the different options offered by the program to sustain their interest.

i) 'Textsalad' - this option is an easy way to start pupils on any text. It prints out the text but with the lines incorrectly sequenced. The pupils simply have to work out or guess which line of text comes first, second, etc. The lines of text are swapped around very easily and no typing is required. In terms of language work the pupils are operating at a level of gist comprehension of the whole passage.

ii) 'Scrambler' - this option converts every word to an anagram. Pupils can work on any word they like. If they type in a correct solution, all occurrences of that word change. Scrambled words appear in upper case for ease of recognition. This option is slightly harder as it requires pupils to work on individual words and requires accuracy in spelling.

iii) 'Prediction' - in this option the pupils are asked to recreate the text, word by word, in its correct sequence. Five choices are offered to the pupil, only one of which is correct. This involves the pupil in thinking about the logical sequence of meaning and word order. It also produced a great deal of debate amongst the pairs.

iv) 'Enigma' - in this option the text is displayed on screen in a coded form. Each letter has been changed to another letter, e.g. f becomes z. Pupils have to work out the code by looking for patterns in the text and a variety of strategies were in evidence. The task seemed almost impossible to many pupils at first but they soon got into the swing of it, helped by the considerable time they had already spent on the text.

There are other options in *Fun with Texts* but the teacher did not use these. Once the pupils had completed the 'Enigma' option they were given a print-out of the text and asked to use it as a template for writing their own self-descriptions. To do this they loaded a word processor. As a variation, they could have used the *Fun With Texts* editor. This is quite cumbersome to use but it does mean that the resultant texts can be used with all the *Fun With Texts* options so that the class could work on the texts created by themselves, perhaps one pair swapping with another.

In this lesson the pupils displayed a high level of concentration, remaining on task with one simple text for almost the whole lesson. They used a wide variety of skills and considered questions of meaning, spelling and structure. They had discussions with a partner about the tasks. They produced something of their own and the quality of this writing clearly demonstrated the value of the work they had done on the computer.

2.4 Hotel form

Pupils carried out a role-play in which one of them took the part of a customer booking into a hotel and the other that of the hotel receptionist. The receptionist had to key in the details of the customer on a computer - much as happens in real life. The teacher used *Minnie* to simulate a hotel registration screen. The blank spaces on the screen could be filled either by typing - useful for the customer's name and address, or by moving words and phrases with the mouse, e.g. types of room, facilities, meals, etc.

The role-play was not completed until the customer's booking details had been printed out and handed to him or her for checking. This simple idea could be used in many other form-filling situations such as changing money, car-hire, booking a holiday, buying a ticket for a journey, etc.

2.5 Vocabulary

Year 7 pupils were introduced to using *Fun With Texts* with a simple vocabulary practice activity. The teacher selected vocabulary which had just been introduced and which had a common theme - food and drink. All the words were given on a particular page of the course book. The twelve words were typed in by the teacher to create a new *Fun With Texts* file. The pupils had to use the 'Enigma' option in *Fun With Texts* which presents words in code. By using the text book the pupils had to guess which words were in the list. Once one word has been correctly identified, the code is partially cracked. This proved to be a fun activity which motivated these pupils to work hard at the task. From a learning point of view, it was a good way to introduce the use of this particular piece of software, whilst as a language learning activity, it gave practice in the vocabulary items which had been introduced but were not yet mastered. It also allowed the pupils to focus on the spellings of the words.

2.6 Menus

A year 8 class listened to a tape of a conversation in a restaurant. The customers first discussed what was on the menu and what they would order before the waiter arrived to take the order. Whilst they listened, the pupils had to note down the various dishes that were mentioned. They then took these notes with them to work on the computer. The teacher had written out the menu as a *Fun With Texts* file. The pupils worked on this using the scrambler option in which the various dishes are presented as anagrams. When they had recast the menu they printed it out and used it to improvise their own role-play.

2.7 House pictures

This is another simple activity which can be used for its own intrinsic value but also as an easy way of introducing pupils to a particular piece of software. A year 9 Italian class learned how to use *Minnie* in this way. The teacher had devised a cloze exercise. The gapped text appeared in the top half of the screen. The bottom half of the screen contained the missing words and some words put in as distractors (see figure 4.3). The text described the interior of a house and the students had a plan of the house to help them work out what the completed text should say. Working in pairs, they used the mouse to move the words from the lower

Figure 4.3

half of the screen to the upper half and fill up the gaps. Once this was finished, the students were given a blank plan onto which they drew various items of furniture. They then redrafted their texts to match the new plan. Having done that, they gapped these texts to recreate a cloze exercise. Different pairs of students then swapped computers to attempt to complete these new cloze exercises. In IT terms the pupils had progressed from the comparatively simple cloze text to the more complex task of redrafting a text. In language learning, they had been able to have extended practice of the structures and vocabulary moving from a simple exercise to one which was more open-ended and they had been able to exercise their imaginations in creating new learning materials for their peers.

2.8 A lesson on travel

A year 9 class in a rural high school. For two consecutive lessons the class had the use of the computer room containing ten computers and an additional workspace. Work had recently begun on third-person report writing using the *passé composé*. After listening to a tape-recording of a dialogue at a booking office supported by visuals in symbol form on OHP, children worked in pairs reproducing the conversation orally. They then continued to work together at the computers using a text manipulation program (*Fun With Texts*). A text, created by the teacher, reported the dialogue in the third person. Pupils first reordered the jumbled lines of text and then recalled it in the form of a cloze exercise in which each group chose the frequency of gapping. Pupils then returned to the work area and created further conversations substituting alternative times, platform numbers and destinations, as well as additional exchanges. In the following lesson, each group used a word processor (e.g. *Folio, Allwrite*) to draft and edit a third-person report based on a cue card. When finished, the report was printed out. Those who finished quickly replaced all occurrences of *il* and *elle* with *je* using the search and replace facility, discussed the resulting text, making any necessary

61

changes appropriate to complete a first person report. As with a number of other case studies, this demonstrates the way in which text manipulation can provide a gentle introduction to text redrafting and, eventually, free writing.

2.9 A hearing-impaired child

A year 8 boy who was otherwise bright had been found to have difficulty discriminating and recognising spoken language. In language lessons he had been given extra practice in listening to audio recordings, but without success. Using a computer running *Fun with Texts* he was able to understand the text heard, owing to the fact that the screen displayed a similar version of the text and he was able to separate and move words around. He has now opted for French in Year 10

Suggested activity

2.10 Secret messages

The 'Enigma' option on *Fun With Texts* could be used to provide a secret message. After decoding this would then be used in some wider task for which the class need to gather information.

3 Using the concept keyboard in modern languages

The concept keyboard on its own is not a panacea, but it provides a different tool for pupils to revise and rehearse the language which is being learnt. It is very unusual for the concept keyboard to be used with a whole group; it is better adapted to small groups of three to four or pair work. Some ideas of group activities and group management are given in the examples below. The concept keyboard enables the pupil to read and write. It is also possible to create activities which involve the other two skills, namely listening and speaking.

3.1 Warehouse

Size of group: three or four. Equipment: one cassette recorder + cassette, one computer + *Prompt/Writer*. Scenario: the pupils are working in a warehouse. Customers have left messages on the answering machine requesting various items. The pupils are to establish and print a list of wanted items to check it at a later stage against the stock list. Monitor: screen is blank at the beginning of the exercise and fills up as the pupils select wanted items. Overlay(see figure 4.4): pictures of the items kept in the warehouse, in this case, clothes.

Tape: e.g.:

  - *Bonjour, je voudrais trois jupes rouges.*
  - *Salut, moi j'ai besoin de six pantalons verts.*

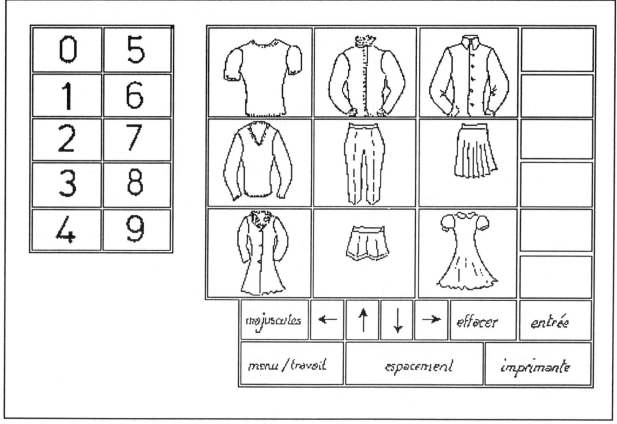

Figure 4.4   Overlay for case study 3.1

3.2 Line reordering

Pupils hear information which is summarised in brief statements. The statements are written in a random order on the overlay. The pupils must decide the order in which they hear the information on the tape by pressing the statements in the same order as the tape. The lines of a poem or a song written in the wrong order are a possibility for such an activity. The example given below is that of a poem.

Group: three or four. Equipment: one cassette recorder + recording of poem, one computer + program *Prompt/Writer*. Scenario: prepare the poem for printing. Overlay: lines of the poem in the wrong order, using half of the space - to allow for a creative writing activity at a later stage. Tape: the poem (either *Un petit chat gris* or another).

3.3 Completing statements

The beginning of the statements are printed on the monitor screen in the order in which they are heard. The end of the statements are written on the overlay in a different order. The pupils place the cursor at the end of the statement they want to complete on the screen and then press the ending they have chosen on the concept keyboard. Size of group: three or four.

Equipment: one cassette recorder + cassette, one computer + program *Prompt/Writer*. Scenario: prepare a summary of the story by completing the beginning of the sentences on the screen with the appropriate endings on the concept keyboard. Overlay: halves of statements. Tape: a story.

3.4 Words with pictures I

Concept match offers an easy random challenge for pupils. Size of group: two pairs. Equipment: one computer + program *Concept match*. Scenario: which pair can find the most correct matches at one go. (Computer to judge, but pairs to keep score as computer cannot do this in this case.) Overlay: pictures of animals.

3.5 Words with pictures II

This time the program used is *Prompt/Writer* and the overlay is blank. Size of group: two or three. Equipment: one Computer + program *Prompt/Writer*. Scenario: the map has just come back from printing, but the printer has not glued the symbols in properly. Please check the computer layout and stick the correct building in the correct places. Overlay: blank - only the background map, but no building. Also required: little cards with pictures of the appropriate buildings.

3.6 Words with pictures III

Using *Touch Explorer Plus* (NCET) to do the version above might break the task down for some pupils or enable higher attainers to attempt a more complex task. Size of group: two or three. Equipment: one computer + program *Touch Explorer Plus*. Scenario: you are the management team of a new hotel. The hotel owner has sent the instructions for furnishing the various rooms on a computer disk. You have an empty plan of the hotel and it is your job to stick the furniture in its proper place. Overlay: the empty plan of the hotel made of felt. The drawings or photos of the furniture have velcro pads on the reverse side so that they can be moved without falling off. File: four different levels: 1)*le sol*, 2) *le(s) lit(s)*, 3) *le cabinet de toilette*, 4) *et aussi?*

Appuie sur le clavier tactile

Dans cette chambre, il y a un lit a deux places et deux lits a une place.

Figure 4.5   **Screen from case study 3.6**

NOTE: The idea of a blank overlay can be pushed further still: place a blank sheet of paper on the concept keyboard and bring real objects into the lesson. The pupils explore the blank piece of paper and place on it the objects as they have been defined in the program. A correction overlay can be provided with the objects drawn or photographs stuck in the appropriate place.

3.7 Literature

Using *Touch Explorer Plus* the main themes of a literary work can be explored. Size of group: two or three. Equipment: one computer + program *Touch Explorer Plus*. Instructions: use the appropriate parts of the program (*dictionnaire, grammaire, mots-clefs,* etc) to help you read the text on the overlay. Using the *notes* facilities, answer the questions in *suppositions*. Overlay: a page from the text which contains clues as to what the main themes of the book are. File: uses the six different levels to provide a dictionary, some guidance about grammar, some guidance about the key-words, some suppositions.

```
Mots-cles  * appuie sur les mots
           * suis les instructions
           * reponds aux questions

SABLE: Indication de l'endroit ou se
          trouve l'auteur.
Utilise la touche "Notes" pour col-
lectionner tous les mots qui se rap-
portent a cet endroit.
```

Figure 4.6   Screen display from case study 3.7

J'étais occupé à éprouver que le soleil me faisait du bien. Le sable commençait à chauffer sous les pieds. J'ai retardé encore l'envie que j'avais de l'eau et j'ai fini par dire: "On y va?" J'ai plongé. L'eau était froide et j'étais content de nager. Avec Marie, nous nous sommes éloignés et nous nous sentions d'accord dans nos gestes et dans notre contentement. Au large, nous avons fait la planche et sur mon visage tourné vers le ciel le soleil écartait les derniers voiles d'eau.	Dictionnaire
	Grammaire
	Mots-clés
	Expressions
	Conclusions
	Suppositions
	Imprimante
	Notes

Figure 4.7   Overlay used for case study 3.7

Mots-cles * appuie sur les mots
           * suis les instructions
           * reponds aux
questions

SOLEIL: symbole de lumiere et de
         chaleur.

Figure 4.8   Screen display from case study 3.7

3.8 Reading to role-play

This activity was used in a semi-rural comprehensive school with a year 9 bottom set - some pupils had special educational needs. This in effect was their second year of learning French as they had not done any French in year 7. Pupils had just done some work on the topic of buying a snack when the overlay used with *Concept match* was introduced. Pupils worked in groups of four with an advisory teacher. (A well briefed *assistant(e)* could fulfil the same function.) The work started with exploring the overlay: first, the pupils offered suggestions as to what the pictures on the overlay represented. Then, as a group of four, they played a straightforward game of *Concept match* (as in case study 3.4) just to verify how correct their suggestions had been. (The program had been set so that both the correct and the incorrect words appeared on the screen and so that the audible reward could be heard.) The advisory teacher read the caption off the screen to support reading and help the pupils associate the words with the sounds. Finally, the speaking game started in earnest: the program was reset so that the audible reward was turned off, but the facility of seeing both the correct and the incorrect words remained. Two pupils faced the monitor and could therefore read what appeared on the screen; they were the customers. The other two pupils, the shop-assistants, could not see the monitor and worked with the concept keyboard and the overlay only. The customers ordered the food which they read off the screen, e.g. *du saucisson*. The shop-assistants pressed the pad they considered to be correct. The customers could check on the screen whether the offered item matched the order, according to the words which appeared on the screen. After about four minutes, the shop-assistants and customers swapped roles.

NOTE: For the same prompt on the screen, the level of language used during this activity can vary according to the level of proficiency of the pupils: e.g. for *du saucisson*, pupils can be encouraged to produce different utterances: *Du saucisson, s'il vous plaît. Je voudrais du saucisson, s'il vous plaît. Avez-vous du saucisson, s'il vous plaît? Auriez-vous du saucisson, s'il vous plaît? Vous reste-t-il du saucisson, s'il vous plaît?* etc.

3.9 Information gap

A group of year 8 bottom set students had just finished, in German, a unit on 'town', which involved both buildings and directions. The aim of the lesson in which the concept keyboard was used was to help them revise for their end of unit test. Two overlays were designed; the symbols used were the same on both, but they were placed in different blocks. One of the overlays was for *Concept match*, the other was for *Prompt/Writer*. The latter was a collection of blank boxes. At the same time, small symbol cards - the same size as the blank boxes on the overlay - were made up. A correction overlay was also compiled, with the symbols stuck in the correct blocks. The first stage of the lesson was to make the whole class make suggestions as to what the symbols could mean by drawing them on the blackboard and playing a few whole class games without the computer. For the second and third stages, the class was divided into four groups of five: twice two teams of five. The second activity involved the pupils in playing the speaking game described in the previous case study with *Concept match*. But, to make the activity more purposeful, the number of correct responses each team gave before making a mistake were counted, and the team with the most correct consecutive answers scored one point, the second two points, etc. The final stage involved the use of the blank-boxed overlay with *Prompt/Writer*. Teams were timed and given points as before. One team had the blank-boxed overlay and the small cards. The other team saw the monitor screen. The first team pressed a blank cell and asked *Was ist denn das?* The other team read the answer off the screen and the first team placed the small card they thought should be stuck on the empty pad. At the end of the exercise, the 'screen team' checked their opponent's overlay with the self-correcting overlay. Any mistake added two seconds to the team's time.

NOTE: possible extension: If they can produce and understand this level of language, pupils could be asked to handle either definitions or paraphrases of the words which appear on the monitor screen.

3.10 Guessing

Observed with year 10 low attainers French in a comprehensive school. Pupils worked in groups of three or four with the French *assistante* and the overlay *Les métiers*. The *assistante* asked them questions of the type: *Vous êtes infirmier; qu'est-ce que vous portez comme vêtement*. At the beginning, the pupils looked through the data contained in the overlay to produce an answer; the answer could be either the words given on the screen when the overlay was pressed or utterances supported by them. After a little while pupils were encouraged to provide answers without pressing the appropriate pads. These were pressed just to offer confirmation that the answer provided was appropriate. Pupils who could cope with the demand were asked to give more information - colour, size, etc.

3.11 Differentiated role-play

Observed during an in-service session where teachers of modern languages and teachers of special needs were looking at how the computer can support pupils with special educational needs to learn a modern language. Students were given ordinary role-play cards. In a corner of the class room the computer with a concept keyboard and an overlay was available to support the students exploring at varying levels of difficulty, from very simple to demanding. The program used to devise the overlay was *Touch Explorer Plus*. The roles of the hotel receptionist and the customer were available at three levels of language. Each pair decided at which level of difficulty of language they would operate. They could choose to progress to the next level when ready to do so.

3.12 Early writing

Observed in a special school with a group of pupils in years 9 and 10 who were in their second year of learning French. They had two half-hourly lessons a week and were in a small group of approximately eight. The whole sequence described below took several lessons, therefore several weeks. The teacher always used the same overlay (figure 4.9) with two programs: *Concept match* and *Prompt/Writer*. This enabled her to give support and progression in the acquisition of the new language. The presentation stage was done through pictures similar to those presented on the overlay: *J'habite dans une maison, un appartement, une tente, etc.* In another lesson this was recapped and the location was added: *à la campagne, en ville, sur une rivière, etc.* Later on again, the last stage was added: *Je n'habite pas... Je voudrais habiter...* When all the elements had been presented and practised, the overlay was

Figure 4.9

introduced with *Concept match.* The teacher read the captions from the screen and the pupils associated the sound with the pictures. Some pupils who developed reading skills faster than others took the teacher's role in reading from the screen; the game described above in case study 3.8, where some pupils read from the monitor which others could not see, could then be played.

When all pupils were familiar with the connection between the words and the pictures, the next phase, the work with *Prompt/ Writer* could start. The file used with *Concept match* was transferred onto a *Prompt/Writer* disk and pupils could then write where they lived, did not live and would like to live. But some of them did not feel that it was enough to speak about themselves, they wanted to talk about their parents (see figure 4.10), brothers and sisters, and their teacher. So they used their keyboard skills to make their short paragraph into a short conversation between them, asking the question: *David, où est-ce que tu habites?* and the answer which could still be written through the concept keyboard. A case of IT giving freedom to write, even at a very elementary level. (See NCET video part 2 extract 5).

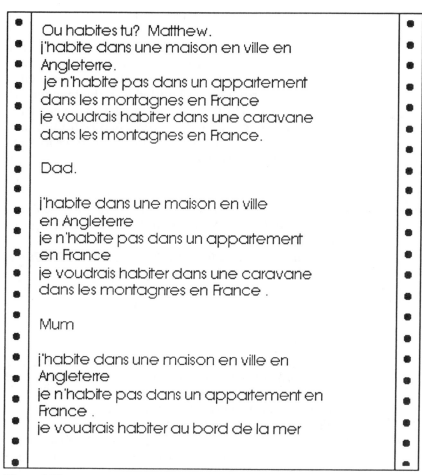

Figure 4.10

3.13 Supported writing

This exercise was used to support sentence construction in a special school for pupils with moderate learning difficulties. Pupils had been doing some work on selected items of clothing, and they had designed some outfits - collages or drawings - using the items they had learnt. The aim of the next piece of work was to describe the outfits in French. The teacher designed a very structured overlay using solely words, and some work was done collaboratively as a whole group of seven to make sure the association between picture, sound and written word was made; this also served to show the pupils how to construct sentences by working systematically from left to right.

3.14 Filling in gaps

This exercise was used with a year 7 mixed-ability group after intensive oral, listening and reading work on personal identity. The following letter was created with *Prompt/Writer* and saved. The missing words were written on the overlay.

> *Guten Tag! Ich ***** *Gisela und ich *** 13 Jahre alt. Ich ***** in Bonn. Bonn ist eine große***** in Westdeutschland. Ich **** einen Bruder. Mein ****** heißt Klaus. Er ist 15 Jahre alt. Ich **** viele Hobbies: Ich **** gern Musik und ich **** besonders gern fern.*

In groups of two or three, pupils completed the letter, saved their own copy, took it to a stand-alone computer where they changed the appropriate words to make it a personal letter which was saved, printed it, submitted it to the teacher, who discussed the work with the individuals, suggested possible improvements and extensions. The letters were then redrafted until the result was satisfactory to all and printed twice: once for display and once for the pupil's exercise book.

> *Ich heisse Rolf. Ich bin 20 Jahre alt. Ich wohne in Hamburg in Norddeutschland. Ich wohne gern in Hamburg.*
> *Ich habe einen Bruder; er heißt Paul; er ist 22 Jahre alt.*
> *Ich höre gern Musik. Ich sehe gern fern.*

Case study 3.14 - letter produced using only the overlay

> *Ich heisse Rolf. Ich bin 20 Jahre alt. Ich wohne in Hamburg; das ist ein großer Hafen in Norddeutschland. Ich wohne gern da; es ist interessant.*
> *Ich habe nur einen Bruder; er heißt Paul; er ist 22 Jahre alt. Er ist nett. Er arbeitet in einer Fabrik.*
> *Ich habe viele Hobbies: Ich habe zwei Lieblingshobbies: ich höre gern Musik und ich sehe besonderes gern fern.*

Case study 3.14 - letter produced using overlay and standard keyboard

3.15 Guided writing

This activity was used in a comprehensive school with a year 9 group learning German as a second foreign language as one of the tasks in a circus of activities. The overlay gave pupils the opportunity of writing a letter which was fairly open-ended, even though it was heavily supported. The pupils were encouraged to use the ordinary keyboard and used any word or phrase they felt confident about and which was not provided on the overlay.

3.16 Creative writing

In a school where the computer room was kitted out with six concept keyboards, an advisory teacher worked with a group of twelve children - two per concept keyboard - for two consecutive 35 minutes lessons. The creative writing was the last stage of intensive work on a poem. The whole of the work was done using the concept keyboard. The pupils started by exploring meaning through the medium of *Concept match*. The overlay used was a graphic reproduction of the poem. The pupils, working in pairs, were then asked to listen to the poem and to place the lines back in order. Finally, they were made to use the *Find and change some words* facility of the word-processor to change:

- the name of the animal;
- the colour of the animal;
- the action the animal was doing;
- the place where it was;
- the person who was talking to it.

Finally, the test was to see if the rhythm of the poem was still the same as that of the original. If not, then changes needed to be made. Some pupils asked if they could choose other animals - that was allowed, of course. Another example of how a very supported activity can fire the imagination of the pupils.

NOTE: similar activities can be done with songs. A year 11 high attainers group filled in missing lines in the folk song *Combien t'ont-ils coûté tes jolis sabots?* and were then asked to create a song which could still be sung on the same tune, but using modern items of clothing - the support offered by the overlay enabled students to make sense of the agreement with the preceding direct object.

Suggested activities

3.17 What was the

question?

A group of four pupils sat around a computer and a concept keyboard; the overlay used has a series of blocks marked Q1, Q2, Q3, etc which hide questions, some of them requiring similar answers; another set of blocks provides words and phrases answering the questions. The pupils worked in two pairs: pair A could only see the monitor and asked the questions as they appeared on the screen. Pair B answered each question by reading the appropriate block and by pressing it. Pair A decided whether the answer provided was suitable (*Oui, d'accord!*) or not (*Non!* and they repeated the question). When Pair A got the answer *Oui, d'accord*, they said *Une autre question?* and pressed another question block. Pairs swap roles after five minutes.

71

3.18 Role-play

Size of group: three or four. Equipment: one computer + *Touch Explorer Plus.* Scenario: one person is operating the concept keyboard and sees the monitor screen. He or she is the *Serveur/ Serveuse.* The other three persons are the customers and their role is to find out what drinks are on offer and order them. Monitor screen shows whatever information is required according to which pad has been pressed. Overlay: has pictures of the drinks on offer plus cues for the possible information available for each drink: *boissons, renseignements, plus de renseignements, prix, etc*

NOTE: this could be made into a listening comprehension exercise by using the Speech facility in the program: the *serveur/ serveuse* has lost his/her voice and can only communicate with the customers through the computer's voice.

Summary

The concept keyboard has a lot of potential to support the learning of a modern foreign language at all levels. It does not need to be limited to the sole skills of reading and writing as it can greatly enhance the development of the other two skills. In modern languages, the concept keyboard has long been associated with supporting pupils with special educational needs; it does provide alternative activities to record understanding of spoken or written texts; it does take away the drudgery from writing and frees the children to concentrate on what they want to write rather than how they are going to write it. But, by being creative when designing the activities and the overlay, it is possible to unleash the children's imagination and to enable them to become more adventurous and creative.

4 Databases

Databases are best described as electronic filing cabinets. Information can be stored according to very clearly defined categories and can be retrieved easily through looking at keywords. We, modern languages teachers, can be instrumental in delivering and assessing the IT capability related to information handling in so far as databases can be used very effectively in our classrooms.

(Note: the software used in the first three case studies cannot be called a database in so far as the users cannot effect a search against a keyword, neither can they enter new information; the software does not afford the possibility of creating a new collection of information. Nevertheless, it is still useful to equip pupils with the idea of information being stored in an electronic filing cabinet and that an electronic file can be read to extract needed information.)

4.1 Databanks I

A year 9 bottom set were revising food and restaurants; the point of using the databank *Au restaurant* (RLDU) was to reinforce the work they had done in the previous lessons. The work with the databank was to take place in the computer room; so, before the lesson the teacher had prepared enough disks and worksheets for each of the groups described below to have one. The pupils had been required to come to their normal teaching room where they were to be briefed. They were to work in groups of three around one computer. Each group would nominate a leader who would collect the disk and the worksheet as they entered the computer room. The worksheet would require members of the groups to make decisions. These decisions had to be agreed by all before they could be entered on the sheet. All groups would have to wait until everybody was ready so that the first two or three questions could be worked through together. The pupils were not at this point told that they would be challenged to more by the worksheet when they reached the end of it. The groups were formed and leaders appointed before the class went to the computer room. On entering the room, group leaders collected the disk and worksheet for their group. Groups settled down around computers. The programs were loaded and the first two questions were tackled by the class as a whole; this ensured that there were no problems in knowing what was required of the pupils both in terms of IT and in terms of language. The classroom became a hive of activity, groups were flicking through electronic pages, sometimes using combinations which tended to be rather long-winded, but usually finding the solution to the problems posed on the worksheet. A few groups asked for support once or twice, often needing reassurance rather than real help. After a while, individuals came and asked the teacher whether they could attempt 'route 2'. This was granted. The whole class was on task for the whole of the sixty minutes they spent in the computer room; they read and re-read words they might have glossed over had they been written on a piece of paper. They were actively reading, solving problems.

4.2 Databanks II

The same software was used on a refresher course for teachers of modern languages as part of an introduction to IT in the modern languages classroom. This time the worksheets were not used, but cassettes were recorded emulating the types of messages which would be left on an answering machine in a *Syndicat d'Initiative*. The teachers worked in pairs; each pair was provided with a small cassette recorder, a cassette and a disk where all the databanks had been collected and for which a special menu had been written. They listened to the recordings, decided what each customer wanted, searched the appropriate databanks to investigate possible solutions to the customers' queries. The last part of the task involved writing memos to the customers.

The whole activity can be differentiated for three skills:

listening - the task can be made more or less demanding by modifying the complexity of the demands of the customers, the complexity of the language used, the speed and manner of the delivery

reading - the demands made on the pupils in terms of reading will need to be set before the tapes are recorded; some items of the databank are less difficult than others. An audit of the language on screen will need to be made before the tape is written and recorded

writing - lower attainers could have been asked to fill in a simple proforma already designed for them; other students might have been given a more open task by which they had to design and fill in the proforma using their own knowledge of the language to its maximum; the higher attainers would be required to write the customers a full letter

IT - the whole task could also be done in a differentiated manner in terms of IT. Students performing on a lower level of IT competency could have called up the proforma to complete the screen and then they could have filled it in. More advanced students might have been asked to design their own proforma using a word processing or a desk top publishing package and fill it in. At a higher level of IT competency, students should be given the opportunity to select the software they consider most appropriate for the task in hand. Designing the proforma and writing the letter would lend themselves well to this sort of differentiation.

4.3 Databanks III

Observed with a year 10 middle ability set in a comprehensive school. Pupils had just revised hotels for the module on which they were working. While the whole class were working on a circus type activity, pairs of pupils left the classroom to go and work with the computer and with the assistante. They used one of the situations given on the second side of *route 4* (English version). As instructed on the worksheet, one of them played the part of the employee at the tourist office, the other acted on behalf of potential customers. The tourist office employee could see the screen and operated the computer to answer the customer's queries who could not see the screen but had to negotiate all the items on his/her task card. The possible hotels had to be investigated and the most appropriate one selected together. The *assistante's* role was to act as support when conversation slackened or words failed the two protagonists. On the whole the conversations did not take very long - four to seven minutes. To give as many pupils as possible the opportunity of acting out the simulation, it had been agreed that the reversal of roles would not happen immediately, but the next week if all pairs managed in one week or, if not, later on in the year with a similar activity.

This activity could have been extended by asking pupils to draw or write their own circumstances and the facilities they would like to find in a hotel. The conversation could have then be carried out as before, but using their own parameters as stimulus.

(Note: the databanks in themselves do not offer much scope in terms of IT competency, but the same sort of retrieval work could be set up on information entered in a database. Students could then practise - and possibly be assessed on - doing simple and/ or complex searches.)

74

4.4 Robbery

In a year 10 class, pupils are revising personal identity and physical descriptions. They are working in groups of four or five around the theme *On recherche*. A series of bank robberies have happened in a small town. Several reports on the sightings of the robber are available on cassette. There are recordings of reports from three different witnesses, largely concurring but with a few minor differences, all three reports are incomplete. As written evidence, there are letters from friends who witnessed one of the robberies and press reports. Yet again, the reports largely concur, but present some minor differences and are incomplete. A police database is set up in a corner of the classroom and is available as and when the pupils feel they need to search it. Some cue cards offer the opportunity to prepare questions to ask potential witnesses. Pupils work through the aural and written information they are given. When they feel that they have a precise enough description, they are free to interrogate the database, asking for instance to list all the people over 1.70 metres, with long blond hair and green eyes. The computer will list all the people who answer this description; pupils will have to look at the other features of these people and return to the reports to find clues which might enable them to narrow the search down. When the pupils are given only one person by the database, they print the police record and make a *On recherche* poster. This poster can be done by hand or using a simulation package like *Quelle tête*; the picture obtained will need to be accompanied with a description written out in full.

4.5 East Enders

A database was set up using the software which can be activated from the concept keyboard: *List Explorer* (NCET). The class, a year 10, needed to revise known family relationships and introduce other types of relationships, particularly those relating to the extended family and boyfriends and girlfriends. To set up the database, the teacher had chosen to use characters from well-known TV soap operas. Some mistakes were slipped into the better known relationships, e.g. *Peter Beale, le père de Pauline Fowler* whilst others were correct, e.g. *Arthur Fowler, le beau-frère de Peter*. Leaving the main classroom activities (reading and listening in connection with their outcome at the end of the unit of work, i.e. creating the storyboard for their own soap opera), pupils visited the concept keyboard in pairs and were given the brief to verify the information stored in the database and check, using a dictionary if need be, any vocabulary they were unsure of and note it down. Once the three pairs had done the work on the concept keyboard, they formed a group of six which could proceed in planning the characters in their soap and the relationships between them.

4.6 Dictionary

Observed with a year 9 class, during a reading lesson. Pupils had to read different texts for pleasure. The rare words in the texts had been entered by the teacher in *MLFind*[1], French version. The fields chosen were *Français, Type, Anglais* and *Sort*. The database became a dictionary which children could access by spelling the

---

[1]For details on *MLFind* write to R Blamire at NCET (address in appendix 3).

French word whose meaning they wanted to find. A database can also be used as a reference source, not only to take the place of a dictionary, but also instead of a verb table, which can list the tenses which the pupils need to understand and handle. This sort of support is particularly important for pupils who cannot handle the conjugated/declined forms of the verbs/words. It is also more user friendly as the 'includes' search enables the pupils to find the meanings of words which they do not necessarily spell properly.

4.7 Holidays

The class had been studying the topic of holidays and learning the future tense. A natural progression was to conduct a survey to find out pupils' own plans. The class decided on the questions they wanted to answer (e.g. which country people are going to, which month, how long, what they intend to do) and set up a computer database to receive the results. Pupils then moved between three activities:

(1) a pair of pupils interviewed other pairs and recorded their answers on data collection sheets;
(2) groups transferred the information onto the database, editing the data so that it was in a standard form; one pupil spoke the information, another typed it in and a third checked the details;
(3) groups wrote down in their exercise books the answers they expected, e.g. the most popular month will be August, most people will go to Spain, etc.

Once the details were stored in the database, they were printed out as pie charts and graphs, which pupils took away for reporting back. Other groups in other lessons could then extract information from the computer and use it in their work. Using the computer made the pupils realise the need for awareness of purpose and accuracy, and provided a meaningful, stimulating, 'adult' outcome for their work. (NB: this lesson is documented on NCET information file 6. Some details have been altered.)

4.8 Was machst du, wenn es ... ?

A year 10 group mixed ability had just finished learning the weather and the leisure activities in German. The teacher built a database where the field names read:

1. *Warm*
2. *Kalt*
3. *Regen*
4. *Schnee*
5. *Wind*

The pupils have rehearsed the questions: *Was machst du, wenn es ... ?* They have also practised their answers. The lesson took place in the computer room: the class had been divided into three equal groups, A, B and C. Pupils in groups A and B were paired off and they were going to ask the questions and operate the computer as a pair. Members of group C were going to move from computer to computer, in order to answer the questions. All this was apparently happening at random, but the teacher had made sure that pupils who had difficulties with the questions would be paired with somebody who could support them. After every member of group C had answered the questions, groups A and C manipulated the computer and group B answered the questions and finally, it was the turn of groups B and C to interrogate group A. Towards the end of the lesson, most computers should have had exactly the same information. Was it really the case? Groups of three (determined by the pairs A + B, B + C and A + C) worked in front of the computers: they were asked to collate the information they had accrued by drawing pie-charts of their results, using the graph program of the database. The pie charts were printed and displayed in the classroom. The discrepancies were observed. They, of course, depended on the sample each group had been able to interrogate in the time allowed.

4.9 Twin town

Organisation : *Pratten*
Anschrift : *Charlton Road, Midsomer Norton, BA3 4AG*
Tel. Nummer : *(0761) 41????*
Bedienungen : *Fabrik*
Besetzer : *BM Gruppe*
Öffnungszeiten:
 Büro: *9.00 bis 17.30*
 Fabrik: *7.30 - 17.30*
Auskunft : *Fenster, Türen, Treppen wurden hier hergestellt.*

A year 10 class was working on a module of work which involved them presenting their town to the twinning committee of a German town. The class was working in six groups of five, each group presenting their findings in a way they felt appropriate. One group decided to investigate the possibility of setting up a database about their own town in German. They decided for themselves on the shape the records would have, on the number of fields they would include and on the names of the fields. The fields were as follows: *Organisation, Anschrift, Tel. Nummer, Bedienungen, Besetzer, Öffnungszeiten, Auskunft.* They then proceeded to enter the information they had collected in the community (see illustration). They then sorted (i.e. classified) the information they had collected according to the various types of services offered. The information was printed out and graphs produced for display purposes. In this last case study, the students yet again selected the piece of software they felt was most appropriate for the work they wanted to do; they designed the database and entered the data themselves.

Summary

Databases are a powerful tool which can enhance work in all of the modern foreign languages skills. The use of databases in foreign language learning probably generates more use of the language than any other application. The case studies above show that a database can profitably be used for reading, speaking and writing; there is no reason why it could not be used for entering responses to listening comprehension; the scenario for a listening task could be: you are a secretary in a survey office; a team of reporters has interviewed people in the streets of St. Julien. These people have been asked what sort of facilities they would like in their town for shopping, entertainment, sport. Enter the responses they give in the database. A database is very versatile and can serve the modern language teacher both in the classroom and in his/her administrative tasks. It can also produce a format for information gap exercises since it is straightforward to print empty records and thus give a framework to a child who has to elicit information from a partner who has the same proforma filled in.

5 Electronic mail

5.1 Faxday

Year 11 classes within ten different schools in one LEA held a Faxday. Each school had to have a Fax machine in order to participate. In the weeks leading up to the Faxday, the pupils worked to produce items for a news sheet consisting of three A4 size pages. Items included cartoons, local news and sport, jokes, stories, poems and features. All schools used word processing for some of the items and desk top publishing for titles and headlines. However, the final products were cut and pasted together by more traditional methods. On the Faxday itself, each school faxed their three sheets to the nine other schools. The faxing was completed in a pre-arranged three hour period and the expense was minimal given that each school had to make only nine local calls, none of which exceeded three minutes. As a result, each school now had a thirty page newspaper. A great deal of interest was shown in the incoming news sheets which were critically appraised in terms of layout, illustration and content. In some schools the completed newspapers were placed in the school libraries where they proved very popular.

5.2 Cross-curricular links

Two schools exchanged the work of pupils in years 8, 9 and 10 in both English and French. The pupils used electronic mail to exchange information on themselves for topics covering personal identity - hobbies, likes and dislikes, etc. They described themselves and exchanged ID cards. In English, the pupils worked collaboratively to produce a story. Later in the year, the link continued as the two schools jointly planned a holiday in France for an imaginary family and used the Fax machine to call tourist offices in France.

5.3 Class exchange

A year 10 class studying Spanish exchanged information with a link class in Spain over the course of a year. Electronic mail could not be used because of compatibility problems - instead they used Fax. The English pupils produced material in English lessons to be sent to Spain. This included a mixture of creative and descriptive writing. The Spanish school sent similar material in Spanish which was used in a variety of ways in the Spanish lessons - for comprehension and as exemplar material for the students own writing in Spanish. It was also used as a stimulus for pupils to write back to in English lessons.

5.4 European Fax

CLEMI, an agency funded by the French Education Ministry, has fostered the development of an international youth magazine which is edited by a host school from copy submitted by other schools by Fax. The first issue appeared in November 1989 and, at the time of writing (June 1991), issue 15 is about to be published. Issue 13 contains articles submitted by schools in Spain, Portugal, Uruguay, USSR, Rumania, Hungary and France. The magazines are predominantly in French but contain articles in other languages. In issue 13, for example, in addition to French, there are articles in Spanish, Catalan, Galician, Portuguese, Hungarian and English. The level of language is quite advanced but varies as some articles are written by native speakers and others by students learning the language at school. Articles may be submitted for future editions and it is possible to be selected as the host school to edit an edition. For more information and to obtain back-copies contact CLEMI (address in appendix 3).

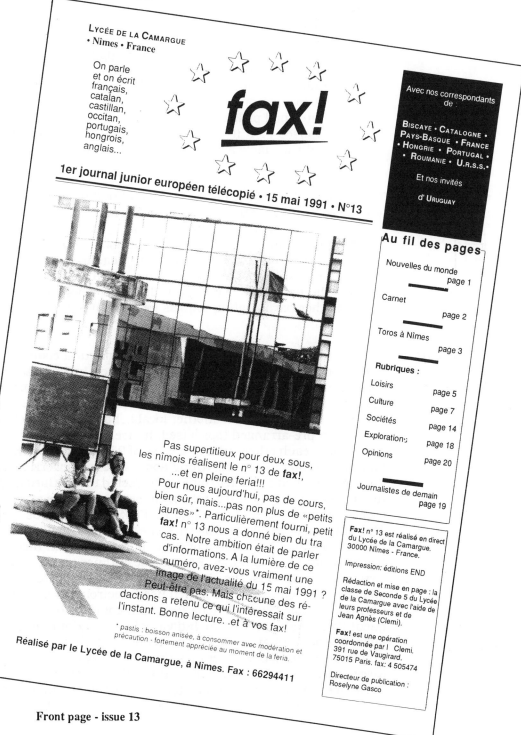

LYCÉE DE LA CAMARGUE
• Nîmes • France

On parle
et on écrit
français,
catalan,
castillan,
occitan,
portugais,
hongrois,
anglais...

fax!

1er journal junior européen télécopié • 15 mai 1991 • N°13

Avec nos correspondants
de :

BISCAYE • CATALOGNE •
PAYS-BASQUE • FRANCE
• HONGRIE • PORTUGAL •
• ROUMANIE • U.R.S.S.•

Et nos invités

d' URUGUAY

Au fil des pages

Nouvelles du monde
page 1

Carnet
page 2

Toros à Nîmes
page 3

Rubriques :

Loisirs
page 5

Culture
page 7

Sociétés
page 14

Explorations
page 18

Opinions
page 20

Journalistes de demain
page 19

Pas supertitieux pour deux sous, les nîmois réalisent le n° 13 de **fax!**, ...et en pleine feria!!!
Pour nous aujourd'hui, pas de cours, bien sûr, mais...pas non plus de «petits jaunes»*. Particulièrement fourni, petit **fax!** n° 13 nous a donné bien du tracas. Notre ambition était de parler d'informations. A la lumière de ce numéro, avez-vous vraiment une image de l'actualité du 15 mai 1991 ? Peut-être pas. Mais chacune des rédactions a retenu ce qui l'intéressait sur l'instant. Bonne lecture...et à vos fax!

* pastis : boisson anisée, à consommer avec modération et précaution - fortement appréciée au moment de la feria.

Réalisé par le Lycée de la Camargue, à Nîmes. Fax : 66294411

Fax! n° 13 est réalisé en direct du Lycée de la Camargue. 30000 Nîmes - France.

Impression: éditions END

Rédaction et mise en page : la classe de Seconde 5 du Lycée de la Camargue avec l'aide de leurs professeurs et de Jean Agnès (Clemi).

Fax! est une opération coordonnée par l Clemi. 391 rue de Vaugirard. 75015 Paris. fax : 4 505474

Directeur de publication : Roselyne Gasco

Front page - issue 13

5.5 The informer

An advanced French class worked on an information gathering exercise. Two computers were linked by cable and the program *Chatter* (NCET NW SEEMERC) . One computer was located in the classroom and the other in an adjacent room. The program gives a split screen display, showing in one half outgoing messages and in the other incoming messages. The pupils worked in groups of three or four at the computer in the classroom. Their task was to interview the foreign language assistant who was using the computer in the other room. They had a number of prepared questions to ask. This activity has advantages over oral interviews - the use of scripted questions is less artificial, the pupils have more time to digest the incoming written answers and may have a written record if a printer is attached, the opportunity for follow-up questions and clarification is still available. Cor sir, how did you program the computer to talk French? was one dazed reaction. A teacher on an INSET day thought that the humble BBC computer had picked up clues to her identity as she typed in her responses as if it were touch-sensitive! These two comments reveal the magic and the realism of IT.

5.6 Newspaper days

These are held regularly on the Campus 2000 network and are advertised in advance there. The electronic mail facility is used to receive news reports. The students' task is to sift through the incoming news and to make editorial decisions such as which stories to run, which stories to lead on, headline writing, sub-headings, redrafting of raw news, lay-out, etc. The final task is to produce the newspaper by a given deadline. This can then be faxed to other participating schools for comparison.

5.7 Links unlimited

The head of modern languages in a large semi-rural comprehensive school had arranged exchanges with a school in Niedersachen, Germany, where a friend of his taught English. Prior to making this link by electronic mail, it was decided to gain experience of using electronic mail with another local school. The two schools decided on pre-arranged topics (self, house, free time, etc) so as not to catch each other out. For a class of 27 it took about 3 x 50 minutes lessons to get everything done. One homework to produce text, a second lesson to type up corrected text, a third lesson to correct corrections and catch any absentees. All the work was saved onto one disk and then sent by TTNS (now Campus Gold). The first package also involved some ordinary mail because photographs had been taken of the children and from these the teacher traced their outlines. From these outlines and the pupils' own self-descriptions, the children in the link school had to try and identify them. The school then used electronic mail with the German school. This was done for initial contacts only. Subsequent links were down to the individual and air/land mail. The link with the German school is now ready to go cross-curricular. Commitment from other faculties has been slow in forthcoming. Nevertheless, the head of languages remains optimistic. The German school already has a Dutch electronic mail link and was hoping to set up a link with Moscow. The English school has a contact with the Ukraine which may develop into a link. Alternatively, the school may join another local project which has links with Oporto and Nijmegen. In this way, the first steps with a school a few miles away have given experience and understanding which can facilitate more ambitious projects.

Suggested activities

5.8 Stations

Mailnet (ILECC) allows for full electronic mail facilities between the different stations in a network room. To get the hang of this application students might devise simple vocabulary tests for each other. A group of two or three students at station 1 sends out a list of five words in the foreign language to a group at station 16. The station 16 group has to send back the meanings of the words in the list in English.

As a next step, the different groups could ask and answer questions in the foreign language. From here it is a short step to devise genuinely communicative activities across the network. Whole class information gaps such as surveys, treasure hunts and jigsaw exercises could be carried out. A partner-finding exercise with cue cards is another possibility.

5.9 Consequences

The following idea for using *Mailnet* has been adapted from an idea on page 94 of Hardisty & Windeatt (1989). It is based on the familiar game of consequences. Working in threes, a class of thirty would occupy ten stations of the network. The teacher begins by giving the first line of a story such as 'One morning John woke up late'. Each group is sent this opening line and then has to add another line in response to a prompt from the teacher such as What happened next? Each group must now send the first two lines of the story to the next station. A new prompt is given and a new line written and so on until the stories are finished. This will usually require at least ten lines so that every group has contributed at least one line to each story. The result is ten different stories which can be sent round to the different stations to be read. Using the electronic mail facility, everyone can read the same story at once. Subsequently, the better stories can be printed out.

6 Miscellaneous

For a variety of reasons, the following case studies have not been grouped into a particular category.

6.1 Police simulation

The following activity was devised for use in initial and in-service training of teachers. It demonstrates a range of task-based IT activities within the context of a simulation. The substantial IT content makes it hard to adapt directly for the school context, but some of the ideas have been successfully used with, for instance, year 9 pupils, as the next case study shows. The simulation is conducted entirely in French, but it is perfectly possible for a few non-speakers of French to participate. The simulation begins with a written briefing document which instructs the participants to form themselves into squads of six to eight detectives and to allocate roles such as finger-print expert, messenger, interrogator, squad leader. The simulation begins with a teletype message reporting a murder. The teletype churns out messages every two or three minutes for an hour thereafter with reports from detectives in the field. The participants use databases of known criminals to search for a match with the incoming descriptions given by witnesses. A concept keyboard overlay is used to match finger-prints which are received by fax. Databases are also used to identify vehicles used by suspects. A supergrass arrives and is interrogated by electronic mail because he/she is fearful of identification (see case study 5.5). As the evidence is built up, one team member is deputed to prepare the case against the prime suspect. This is word processed but it might be preferable to use a program such as *Thinksheet* (Fisher-Marriott) or *Hypercard* to show the links between suspects and clues. The activity is concluded with each team presenting its evidence and denouncing the murderer.

6.2 Identikit

Year 9 pupils worked from a written account of a crime. They used the database of criminals devised for the previous case study, which uses MLFind. Their task was to find the name of a criminal from a written description. They then used *Quelle tête* to produce an identikit picture of the wanted man and printed it out.

6.3 CD Roms

Words can be looked up using an electronic dictionary such as *Le Robert Electronique* - all nine volumes on one CD or *Harrap's Multilingual Dictionary* (Multilingua)- containing seven million words in twelve different languages. Advantages include ease of use. Words are found in the dictionary by typing in the first few letters. Usually only the first two or three are required. Linked words can be viewed automatically. If used in conjunction with a word processor, words and phrases from the dictionary can be pasted directly into the user's text.

6.4 Graphics

Materials and activities were developed for pupils with special educational needs as part of an NCET project. The project team, all teachers or advisory teachers in Northants. LEA, used the program *Collage* (MUSE). Pupils can use the materials to support role-play, for instance, in a café. The screen displays a café scene, with a table, the bar and a menu. Items on the shelves behind the bar can be moved onto the table in response to the customer's order. Similarly, items on the price list can be moved onto the customer's bill at the end of the role play. These bright and attractive materials are fun to use, supportive and highly motivating. (See NCET video part 2 extracts 7 & 9).

6.5 Sound

Pupils used *Hypercard* on the Apple Macintosh. They are guided through a kind of treasure trail by on-screen prompts. At various points they are instructed to press a button which results in some spoken language giving further clues for progress along the trail. Support is available either by repeatedly pressing the button to hear the message over and over. Alternatively, there are help buttons giving translations of some words.

References

Hardisty D & S Windeatt, *CALL*, OUP (1989).
Blamire R & Kayembe (eds), *Look - my language is on the computer*, NCET (forthcoming).

Chapter 5
Planning for the future

In this chapter we will examine ways in which the use of IT in modern languages is likely to develop over the next few years. Will there be more and better computers and is this desirable? What types of software will be available and how will these programs be used? Will IT bring about closer links with other countries? How will teachers adapt to these changes and what will be their impact upon learning? Many of the innovations described are already available but are rarely found in use in modern languages lessons.

New hardware

The pace of change in the field of IT is sometimes frighteningly fast. This point is made by Schofield (1991) who writes:

> 'My six-year old - with an Amiga and hard disk
> attached to the family television, has more power
> than the Pentagon had in the Sixties.'

Not only are there new and more powerful computers, there are other goodies which offer some interesting possibilities. For example, the ability to digitise information (i.e. turn it into electronic form) will make it possible for computers to mix information from video, audio, magazines, newspapers - indeed any information source. However, the excitement of new technology is in stark contrast to the reality of underfunded schools. In some cases the very fabric of the school may be crumbling. Modern languages teachers struggle on with reel-to reel-tape recorders and banda machines. Innovations such as OHPs and videos have not yet been sighted. Thus, in spite of technological advances and in spite of the strong case for using IT in modern languages, it may be that instead of buying more computers modern languages faculties have other priorities. If more computers do become available, they are likely to be computers of the older type, cast off by departments such as maths and computer studies. This may bring within reach the reasonable aim of having one computer per languages room or per languages teacher. These computers may only run simple programs, but tried and tested ones such as *Fun with Texts*, *Granville* and simple teletype emulators such as *Extra!*.

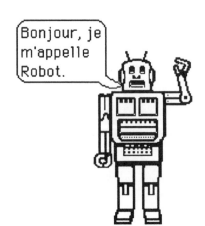

Bonjour, je m'appelle Robot.

In these days of devolved budgets and local management of schools governors may be able to find some funding for additional computers if a good enough case can be made. The strong emphasis on IT in the modern languages National Curriculum helps to make the case. Even if no extra funding can be obtained there should at least be guaranteed access to whole school IT provision which should not be exclusively reserved for computer studies, maths, business studies and science.

Where possible, teachers will want to get their hands on new equipment and, of all possible technological innovations, modern languages teachers will be most interested in those concerned with speech. Already most of the facilities required are available: high quality speech, voice recognition and speech synthesisers. However, they are not, as yet, commonly used in schools. Cheap voice synthesisers have been around for a decade or so. They offer the facility to convert a text to speech. Synthesisers have been developed to cope with the differences in pronunciation between French, German and English. These synthesisers have been used with visually-impaired pupils to give access to some of the features of using computers which they would otherwise be denied. The quality is still somewhat robotic. Although voice recognition is being developed, it is not yet commercially available. The one breakthrough has been in the use of pre-recorded digitised sound to give computers a voice. This facility is available on both Macintosh and PC computers (including RM Nimbus and Archimedes). It is possible to record messages directly onto the computer disk using a microphone or any other source of sound, e.g. directly from a cassette recorder. These messages are then available to be used within a computer program. For example, a treasure trail could be set up. The clues would be sound messages which could be listened to over and over again until understood. Each message would guide the user to the next clue. This would involve using the mouse to make various choices and to move around various screens of information and graphic displays as in a computer adventure. Existing software and hardware make the production of such listening exercises a relatively straightforward, albeit time-consuming, operation. Other listening activities aimed at exploiting this new technology are currently at the developmental stage.

Some resources may become available as a facility for the whole school and modern languages departments need to play their part in determining what should be purchased. Facilities which may be useful include a computer room which is not timetabled and can therefore be booked offering one computer between two pupils for a typical class, an open access computing area located in the library for use as reference and with CD-ROM and modem facilities, a pool of portable equipment for loan such as lap-top computers, printers, concept keyboards, CD-ROMs, etc and a resources centre equipped with adequate desktop publishing facilities for the production of teaching and learning materials and the publishing of pupil work.

6

La seconde planète que j'ai visitée s'appelait la rue des pamplemousses mutilés. La planète était habitée par une majorette qui s'appelait Gertrude McRoggisdedumbon. Elle était chauve, elle avait le nez pointu et elle portait un noeud papillon.

Word-processed creative writing, *Voyage dans l'espace,* by Neil King (year 11) based on his reading of Saint-Exupery's *Le Petit Prince*. The illustrations were added by Robert Davis (year 9) who did not quite get the full meaning of *un noeud papillon.*.

7

Elle a dit "Bonjour"
mais je ne me sentais pas très sociable,
alors j' ai sorti mon fusil - mitrailleur
et j' ai tiré sur la majorette. Elle est
morte avec un cri perçant.

Another page from *Voyage dans l'espace.* **This 16 page booklet is now in the school library along with several others which arose out of the work on** *Le Petit Prince.*

Finally, there is likely to be considerable development in the miniaturisation of computers and pupil access to portable personal machines. At present, one or two highly favoured schools are able to issue every pupil with a lap-top computer. Elsewhere, lap-tops are sometimes provided for pupils with special educational needs; for instance, one deaf pupil in a local school already has such a computer and the school is trying to raise funds to provide another for a year 7 partially-hearing boy. The provision of small personal machines is likely to be an area of expansion. Eventually, all pupils in schools may have such machines. Interim stages may be the acquisition of sufficient computers for a few per class and/or for one whole class. This will open up interesting possibilities for flexible group work using computers. A model for this would be the flexible use of listening stations which is already common in many classrooms.

Another use of lap-tops which is beginning to be seen in schools is for *hoovering* data. Pupils take the lap-top to the central resource bank and collect information from reference computers, perhaps a CD-based encyclopaedia. This is one possibility of the many that will arise from the increased portability of computers.

Software changes

Whilst new applications of relevance to modern languages learning will undoubtedly emerge, it is hard to predict what these might be. What is reasonably certain is that existing applications will be improved so that they work more efficiently, offer new facilities and greater flexibility. If we consider word processing as a case in point, we are likely to see the addition of some powerful facilities. Already, there are spelling checkers and thesaurus facilities. A range of other reference facilities may be added such as bilingual dictionaries, verb tables, encyclopaedia and dictionaries of quotations. Grammar checking software is now becoming available with programs such as *Grammatik* and *Hugo*. These will check a text for basic errors such as adjectival agreements. Users of these packages find that they not only help in the production of grammatically correct texts but also promote learning since they give instant feedback of a non-judgemental kind. In addition to more facilities, a word processor should also become easier to use as software designers strive to make their products more user-friendly and more intuitive. Hopefully, compatibility problems will become a thing of the past and a text produced on any word processor should be useable on any other.

Integrated software Integrated software packages have been available for some time but are becoming much more flexible and efficient. A package might consist of a word processor, graphics program, database, spreadsheet and desk top publishing program. Information from any one can be cut and pasted into any other. A text could be written on the word processor, a graph developed on the database and/or spread-sheet and images built up on the graphics program before bringing together all these elements in the desk top publishing package (this book was produced by using the facilities of sophisticated packages to bring together charts, illustrations and text).

Multi-tasking
Multi-tasking is available on the latest generation of computers such as Apple Macintosh and Archimedes. It allows two or more computer programs to run simultaneously. I found this facility of use to-day when I was compiling a bibliography for student teachers using a word processor. I switched easily to the university's on-line library database to check book details whilst the word processor was left running. This avoids the time and trouble of having to keep loading different pieces of software. It also means that when one switches back to a package it is exactly how it was left. In the modern languages classroom multi-tasking will allow more sophiisticated work-related tasks to be carried out. It will also allow one computer to serve different purposes within one lesson with little or no disruption.

Machine translation
Finally, machine translation is another possibility lurking on the other side of the horizon. In the future our students may be able to type out texts on a word processor which the computer will automatically translate into any desired foreign language. A lot of work has been put into developing such a machine, which would be particularly useful for multi-national companies and large international organisations such as the United Nations and the European Community. However, at present there seems little need for us to revive local branches of the Luddite movement!

The improvement of the various applications currently used in modern languages should widen the scope of their use and enable those teachers currently put off by technical difficulties such as inexplicable breakdowns, to use software with more confidence. The move towards software which is standard in industry and commerce offers the chance of more realism as well as more power and efficiency.

The international dimension

The use of information technology is beginning to lead to the creation of new channels of international communication. The earliest examples were electronic mail and on-line databases such as the French *Minitel*. Much has been said about the usefulness of IT for international communications, in the various National Curriculum documents amongst other places, but there have been obstacles to progress in terms of expense and technical problems to do with compatibility of different systems and differing national standards. In the future, these difficulties are likely to be overcome and this will lead to the creation of new channels of communication. New technologies such as Fax and satellite TV also facilitate international communication and access to foreign information sources. Earlier in this book it was argued that IT represented a new medium for language; dependency upon this medium is likely to increase in the future. *Oracle*, the ITV teletext service, advertises itself as the 'ultimate newspaper'. In the next few years, international communications are likely to be increasingly channelled through the medium of IT.

Computers in disguise

What will the computers of the future look like? One view is that they will become more like television sets. They may well replace video and hi-fi systems and are already threatening to do so in the shape of innovations such as *Commodore Dynamic Total Vision* (CDTV). These machines offer a very versatile home entertainment package incorporating high quality sound and vision. They can also incorporate video games and word processing. The computer of the future may look just like a television set with various remote control hand-held devices for controlling them and entering data. With the home increasingly invaded by IT the classroom will eventually follow.

Conclusion

Whatever the future holds, progress in the use of IT in modern languages is inevitable. As is argued in Chapter 2, it is most likely to be made by those teachers who are developing good practice in other areas of modern languages teaching. Such teachers are able to assess the merits of IT applications in terms of their capacity to enhance learning rather than in terms of technical merit. If such teachers learn to trust their own judgement, then the foolishness of technology for its own sake will be avoided. The dilemma for modern languages teachers is that they must be ready to accept innovation but be vigilant against ill-conceived schemes which distract and undermine language learning rather than support and enhance it.

In the enterprise of integrating IT coherently, teachers will learn with their pupils, for learn must we all about the world of communications and technology, not because it is prescribed as an area of experience within the programmes of study of the National Curriculum, but because it is the world which we now inhabit.

Reference

Schofield J, *Calm amid the Storm*, TES Computers Update p. 28 November (1991).

Appendix 1
Basic tasks

The tasks which follow are some of the routine tasks that must be carried out when using most computers. Once familiar with these basic tasks, it should be possible to cope with the elementary technical problems which may arise during lessons. The tasks are common to both network and stand-alone systems. However, when using a network there will be specific procedures to be learned. These vary according to how the network has been set up and the network manager should provide training in these. The tasks have been clearly defined but a minimum of instruction and explanation has been given. It is expected that help will be sought from manuals or an 'expert'. In working through the tasks it is better to work with someone else of a similar standard in IT terms. Learning together is easier and more fun and reduces the demand on computers, disks, printers and technical advice.

The tasks have been designed to be tackled sequentially and the later tasks depend to an extent upon the earlier ones having already been completed.

(Note: an indication is given of which programs run on which machines but versions are often available for several different machines. If the software required for a task is not available to you there may be other similar programs which will do just as well.)

1 Use a computer

Load a variety of software packages and attempt some of the pupil tasks described in the accompanying notes or manuals.

Suggested software:

Granville (BBC, RM, Archimedes)
Fun With Texts (BBC, RM, Archimedes) - attempt one of the example files on the text salad option
RLDU Mini Databanks (BBC, RM)

2 Use a printer

Use a computer attached to a printer. Load a graphics program that enables a printer to be used. Follow the instructions to produce some work to be printed out. Attempt only one or two of the following suggested programs.

Quelle tête (BBC)
Kopfjäger (BBC)
PaintSpa (RM)
MacDraw 2 (Apple Mac)

3 Format a disk

3.5" disk

Before a new disk can be used it must be formatted. (On the Apple Mac initialised.) WARNING: this process destroys all the information on a disk so do not attempt to format a disk which contains valuable data! Formatting a disk should only be necessary once, although a disk can be reformatted at any time. If a disk is formatted on a BBC computer it will be capable of use only on BBC computers. It is possible to reformat such a disk for use on a different type of machine but this would lose all the data on the disk. On many computers the formatting procedure can be varied to allow more or less data to be stored. Complete the following formatting procedures for the make(s) of computer that you will be using:

BBC computer 5.25" disk 40 tracks
BBC computer 5.25" disk 80 tracks
RM Nimbus computer 3.5" disk
Apple Mac 3.5" disk
PC computer 5.25" disk
Archimedes 3.5" disk

(NB if you have a hard disk be careful not to format it unintentionally!)

4 Wordprocessing 1

Write a brief text using one or more of the suggested programs. Save the text onto the floppy disk formatted earlier. Print out your text. Programs marked with an asterisk have accented characters available and it makes sense to attempt to use these. Keep a copy on disk (i.e. save) of at least one of the texts you create.

*Mac Write** (Apple Mac)
*Minnie** (RM Nimbus)
*Flexiwrite** (RM Nimbus)
*Microsoft Word** (PC etc)
*First Word Plus** (Archimedes)
View (BBC)
Locoscript (Amstrad)
Phases (Archimedes)

5 Checking a disk

A disk can contain a wide variety and a considerable quantity of information. You can easily check if your own work is on a disk by looking at the disk's directory. Follow the instructions for each of the machines.
NB: some files may be located in folders or sub directories. Check manuals for an explanation of how to search these.

RM Nimbus / PC	**BBC**	**Apple Mac**
type *dir*	type *CAT*	insert disk
press RETURN	press ENTER	click on single-sided or doubled-sided
		click on erase
		name the disk

6 Wordprocessing 2

For this task you will need the disk onto which you saved a text for task 4. This task should be started from scratch and not simply continued from task 4, i.e. the text must be reloaded from the disk. Once reloaded, amend the text by correcting spellings, changing words and phrases, adding and deleting. The more adventurous might attempt to move blocks of text, e.g. move the first paragraph or sentence to the end of the text. Save the new text and print.

7 Copying a file

Copy a text file you created in the previous tasks onto a new disk. This must be done without reloading the word processing package and requires the use of a double disk drive computer.

Use the search procedure described in task 5 to check that a copy has been made.

Refer to manual for file copying procedures on other computers, Archimedes, Apple Mac etc.

BBC	**PC/Nimbus**
place original disk in drive 0	place original disk in drive A
place destination disk in drive 1	place destination disk in drive B
type *COPY 01 "filename"*	type *copy a:filename b:*
press ENTER	press RETURN

8 Desktop publishing

Design teaching and learning materials such as flash cards, worksheets, assessment materials, reading materials, OHTs, etc. Your final product should include accented text and graphics (pictures, lines, boxes, shading). Save the work on disk and print it out. Suggested software:

Mac Draw (Apple Mac)
Ovation (Archimedes)
Newspaper (RM Nimbus)
Caxton (RM Nimbus)
Front Page Europe (BBC)
Aldus Pagemaker (Apple Macintosh / PC)

Appendix 2
Tasks for specific programs

1 Concept keyboard

1.1 Using an overlay with Prompt/ Writer on the BBC

place your disk in the disk drive

press shift/break

press S to check start-up conditions

ensure the start-up conditions match your equipment, change if necessary

P/W start-up conditions	Page 1

Continue with the conditions as set

Check other conditions page
See the HELP pages
Ignore changes and leave

Disc drive	Single
Screen letter size	Single

Printout
Letter size	Double height
Left margin	20 chars
Page length	66 lines

Space bar to move	RETURN to select

Start-up conditions screen

when the conditions match your set-up, select
CONTINUE WITH CONDITIONS AS SET

press RETURN

choose P for Prompt (one page of text) or
W for Writer (a longer document)

**1.2 To make an over-
lay for Prompt/
Writer on the BBC**

place disk 2 in the disk drive

press shift/break

press S to check start-up conditions

ensure the start-up conditions match your
equipment and change if necessary

P/W Utility Disc start-up conditions

Continue with conditions as set

See the help pages

Ignore any changes and leave

Disc drive   Single

Printer type   Epson FX80
Printer connection   Parallel
Printer linefeed   On

**Start-up
conditions
screen for
utility disk**

when the conditions match your set-up, select
CONTINUE WITH CONDITIONS AS SET

press RETURN

select MAKE AN OVERLAY

press RETURN

overlay conditions page: these conditions are
probably best left as follows:
Editor squares = yes
Space after message = yes
Type of overlay = irregular
press RETURN to continue

name your overlay (up to 7 characters)

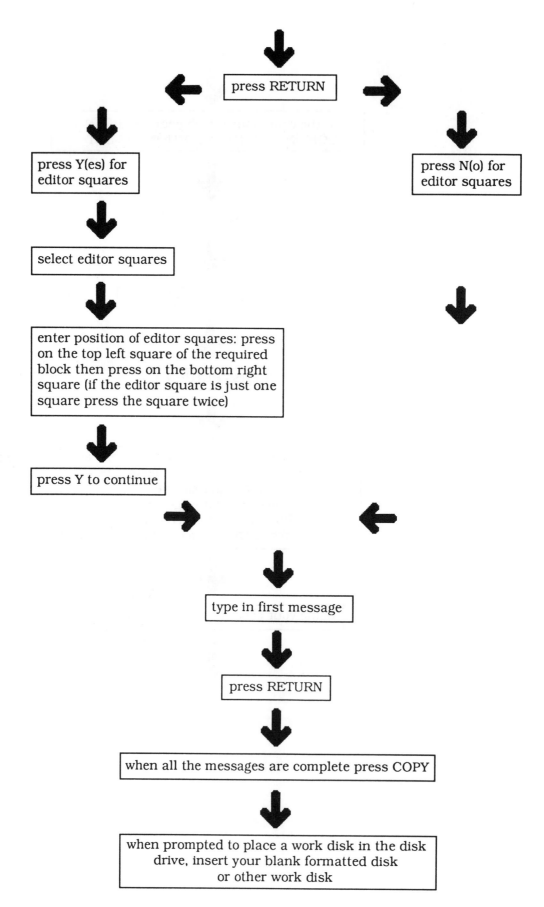

1.3 Using an overlay with Concept Match on the BBC

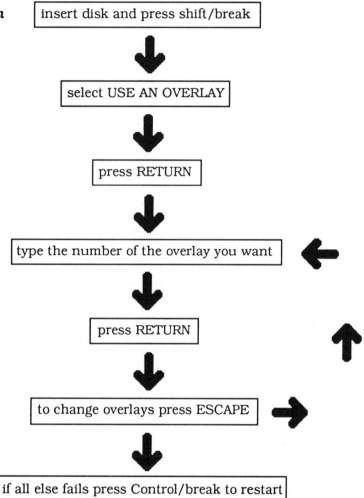

insert disk and press shift/break

↓

select USE AN OVERLAY

↓

press RETURN

↓

type the number of the overlay you want ←

↓

press RETURN ↑

↓

to change overlays press ESCAPE →

↓

if all else fails press Control/break to restart

**1.4 Using an overlay
with Touch Explorer
Plus on the BBC**

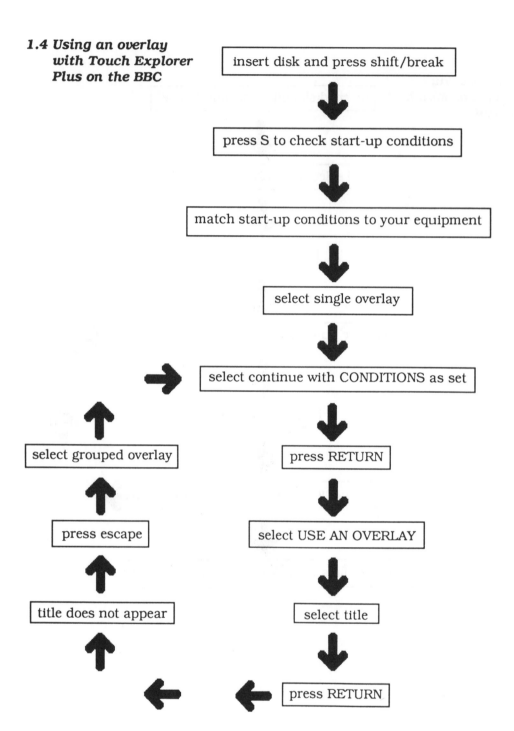

insert disk and press shift/break

press S to check start-up conditions

match start-up conditions to your equipment

select single overlay

select continue with CONDITIONS as set

select grouped overlay

press RETURN

press escape

select USE AN OVERLAY

title does not appear

select title

press RETURN

2 Tasks for Minnie (RM Nimbus)

2.1 Reviewing pupils'
work

from main menu highlight LOAD SOME TEXT
FROM THE DISK

↓

click mouse OR press RETURN

↓

highlight a file ⬅

↓

click mouse OR press RETURN ⬆

↓

use arrow keys or page down to read text

↓

to load another text move mouse until tip of
mouse pointer is over the smiling face in the
bottom right of the screen ⬆

↓

click mouse OR press RETURN ➡

2.2 To write a new text

from the main menu highlight and click on START SOME NEW TEXT

highlight and click on YES

return to main menu

highlight and click on LOAD A WORD FILE FROM THE DISK

highlight and click on a word file

click on one of the four colour boxes to see a list of words / phrases

highlight and click on a word or phrase to move it into your text

build up a text typing in as few words as possible

2.3 To set up accents

```
┌─────────────────────────┐
│    return to main menu  │
└─────────────────────────┘
```

```
┌─────────────────────────┐
│   highlight and click on │
│     USE THE UTILITIES    │
└─────────────────────────┘
```

```
┌──────────────────────────────────────────────┐
│ from the utilities menu: highlight and click on │
│            CHANGE THE SETTINGS                  │
└──────────────────────────────────────────────┘
```

```
┌──────────────────────────────┐
│    highlight and click on     │
│  FUNCTION KEY CHARACTERS      │
└──────────────────────────────┘
```

```
┌──────────────────────────────┐
│ highlight and click on a language │
└──────────────────────────────┘
```

```
┌──────────────────────────────┐
│    highlight and click on     │
│  RETURN TO THE MAIN MENU      │
└──────────────────────────────┘
```

```
Function key templates

French          German          Spanish

F1  à           F1  ä           F1  á
F2  Ç           F2  Ä           F2  é
F3  è           F3  ö           F3  í
F4  ç           F4  Ö           F4  ó
F5  ì           F5  ü           F5  ú
F6  é           F6  Ü           F6  ü
F7  ò           F7  ß           F7  ñ
F8              F8  à           F8  Ñ
F9  ù           F9              F9  ¿
F10             F10             F10 i

  With shift

F1  â           F1              F1  Pt
F2  «           F2              F2
F3  ê           F3              F3
F4  »           F4              F4
F5  î           F5              F5
F6              F6              F6
F7  ô           F7              F7
F8              F8              F8
F9  û           F9              F9
F10             F10             F10
```

Templates for *Minnie*

2.4 To create a
word file

There is some thinking to do first. What are the students going to write about and at what level? Will they start with a blank page or with the first paragraph already done? How will the different coloured boxes be used - grammatically, semantically or sequentially? These need not be major considerations for a first attempt since a simple idea will do for starters. For example, the pupils will be asked to design and print out menus, you just need to type in dishes for each of the different courses from which they will choose. A different coloured box for each course will help them to correctly structure their menus. It is a good idea to work out ideas on paper and to keep a note of what is entered on the computer.

> from the main menu highlight and click on
> USE THE UTILITIES

> highlight and click on
> CREATE A NEW WORD FILE

> for each colour (red, green, blue and yellow)
> follow steps in shaded boxes

highlight and click on EDIT ... SET (RED, etc)

move tip of mouse pointer into top blue box

position brown highlight for first word or phrase

click to get yellow dash then enter word or phrase

press RETURN

repeat until page is full

highlight and click CHANGE GROUP

until this set is complete

highlight and click END CHANGES

highlight and click YES

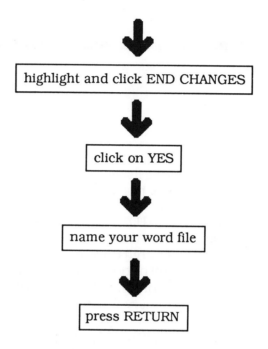

Appendix 3
Addresses

The following list of addresses includes the publishers of many of the software packages referred to in the text:

AVP, School Hill Centre, Chepstow, Gwent NP6 5PH

Camsoft, 10 Wheatfield Close, Maidenhead, Berkshire SL6 3PS

CUP, Edinburgh Building, Shaftesbury Rd., Cambridge CB2 2RU

Claris International, 1 Roundwood Avenue, Stockley Park, Uxbridge, Middlesex UB11 1BG

DFE, Sanctuary Buildings, Great Smith Street, Westminster, London SW1P 3BT

ESM, Freepost, Abbeygate House, East Rd., Cambridge CB1 1BRESM, Freepost, Abbeygate House, East Rd., Cambridge CB1 1BR

Fisher-Marriott, 3 Grove Road, Anstey, nr. Coventry CV7 9JD

FLIP Project, Languages Centre, Modern Languages Building, PO Box 147, Liverpool L69 3BX

ILECC, John Ruskin St., London SE5 0PQ

IT Service, Bilford Rd., Worcester WR3 8QA

Jean Agnès Clémi, 391 rue de Vaugirard, Paris 75015

Language Centre, St Martin's College, Bowerham Rd., Lancaster LA1 3JD

Multilingua, 61 Chiswick Staithe, London, W4 3TP

MUSE, PO Box 43, Houghton on the Hill, Leics. LE7 9GX

NCC, Albion Wharf, 25 Skeldergate, York YO1 2XL

NCET, Science Park, Coventry CV4 7EZ

Nelson and Co., Mayfield Road, Walton on Thames, Surrey KT12 5PC

NERIS, Maryland College, Leighton St., Woburn, Milton Keynes MK17 9JD

Newman Software, Newman College, Genner's Lane, Birmingham B32 3NT.

Northwest SEMERC, Fitton Hill CDC, Rosary Rd., Oldham OL8 2QE

RLDU, Sheridan Rd., Horfield, Bristol BS7 0PU

SECC, Floor 7, Unity House, Hanley, Stoke-on-Trent, ST1 4QP

Sherston Software, Swan Barton, Malmesbury SN16 0LH

SPA, PO Box 59, Leamington, Warks., CV31 3QA.